T0338902

THE CURE
FOR OUR BROKEN
POLITICAL PROCESS

THE CURE
FOR OUR BROKEN
POLITICAL PROCESS

*How We Can Get Our Politicians to Resolve
the Issues Tearing Our Country Apart*

Sol Erdman & Lawrence Susskind

Potomac Books, Inc.
Washington, D.C.

Library of Congress Cataloging-in-Publication Data
Erdman, Sol.
 The cure for our broken political process : how we can get our politicians to resolve the issues tearing our country apart / Sol Erdman & Lawrence Susskind. — 1st ed.
    p. cm.
 Includes bibliographical references and index.
 ISBN 978-1-59797-269-7 (alk. paper)
 1. Political participation—United States. 2. Politicians—United States. 3. United States—Politics and government—21st century. I. Susskind, Lawrence. II. Title.
 JK1764.E73 2008
 320.60973—dc22
                              2008020945

Printed in the United States of America on acid-free paper that meets the American National Standards Institute Z39-48 Standard.

Potomac Books, Inc.
22841 Quicksilver Drive
Dulles, Virginia 20166

First Edition

10 9 8 7 6 5 4 3 2 1

CONTENTS

Introduction

The Change That Can Transform Our Political Life

America is in peril. The signs are all around us: Our government is piling up enough debts to ruin us financially within a generation. Most of our children receive second-rate educations. Millions of our fellow citizens are losing their homes in foreclosures. We are consuming record amounts of foreign oil, thereby enriching countries intent on harming us. Global warming threatens to scorch our farm belt and flood our coastal cities. Our health care costs are soaring—growing twice as fast as our incomes. Our standing in the world has plunged. And rogue nations are obtaining nuclear weapons that could imperil world stability for the indefinite future.

Yet instead of grappling with these problems, our politicians battle mostly with one another. As one governor's wife put it, the members of Congress act like "two guys in a canoe that is headed for the falls, and all they do is hit each other with their paddles." Those two guys, though, have the power to drag the entire country over the precipice with them.

What can any of us do about it? Plenty—once most of us truly understand why our politicians behave the way they do.

To see what we mean, we need to tell you about our experience as mediators—and what it has revealed to us about American politicians. We referee conflicts among warring interest groups, government agencies, businesses, communities, and, occasionally, nations. The adversaries we've worked with have often started out angrier than typical politicians. Yet most of those adversaries have also wanted to stop wasting their time and money on endless battles. So they've sat down with their enemies face-to-face to search for a possible deal.

1

Many of them have succeeded. We've helped diplomats from around the world agree unanimously on how to slow down global warming. We've watched environmentalists and business titans reach agreement on how America could best meet its ravenous need for energy.

In fact, for nearly every major national problem that elected politicians are *still* fighting over, we know of ideological enemies who negotiated a practical solution that all sides endorsed. Those adversaries then presented their solution to elected politicians—who ignored it. The politicians just kept on feuding. We've seen this sequence occur time after time. Finally, we realized what drives elected politicians to behave so destructively.

Elections—the way they're organized today—are the main culprit. Look at just one feature that nearly all of us take for granted but that ends up sabotaging American political life: In nearly every election, a Republican and a Democrat compete for the seat. One party wins, while the other party loses. How, then, can we expect Republicans and Democrats in Congress to spend much time working together? That would be somewhat like expecting two prizefighters, while competing for a championship, to stop throwing punches—and start waltzing. Sure, the two parties cooperate occasionally. But much like two boxers shaking hands, that gesture lasts but a moment and is mainly for show. Each lawmaker knows that to win the next election he or she will have to knock the challenger from the other party out of contention. So, most lawmakers bash the opposing party at every opportunity.

Most troubling of all, these verbal attacks succeed. Over the last decade, as our lawmakers have relentlessly blamed one another for our nation's troubles, while allowing those troubles to grow worse, 97 percent of those lawmakers who've run for reelection have held onto their seats. Nearly every member of Congress has thereby seen firsthand that he or she can win election after election just by spotlighting the other party's failures.

So, as long as our elections work as they do today, our lawmakers will undercut one another every chance they get. Our chronic problems will therefore continue to plague us. Our energy and health care costs will keep on soaring. Our government will continue to spend recklessly. Most of our kids will continue to receive mediocre educations. And so on.

Many of us believe that we could avoid this grim future if our fellow citizens would just choose the right president. But even the most eloquent and politically astute president could not overcome the perverse incentives in our congressional elections that drive our lawmakers to sabotage one another. So, no matter who is president, Congress will continue to bungle issue after issue—until we design its elections differently.

The obvious question is: Can we structure our elections so that, to win, a lawmaker would have to negotiate genuine solutions to our urgent problems? In this book, you'll see that the answer to that question is yes.

We first realized that goal was within reach after years of watching ideological opponents hammer out practical solutions to issues they had spent their careers fighting over. From these experiences, we saw what it would take to coax elected politicians to work in the very same way. We saw how to organize elections so that each politician would want to resolve his or her differences with opposing camps as sensibly as he or she could.

The core concept is simple: Now, one Republican and one Democrat compete head-on to fill each district's one House seat. Imagine, instead, if each district had several House seats, with three or more liberal candidates competing to represent the district's liberal voters, while at least three conservative candidates competed to represent the district's conservative voters, several moderates competed to represent the moderates, and so on. In that kind of election, each lawmaker would no longer have to defeat a challenger on the opposite end of the spectrum. So he or she would have no reason to bash lawmakers opposite him or her on the spectrum. On the contrary, to keep his seat, each lawmaker would have to convince his voters that he'd accomplished more of their agenda than would the two other candidates ideologically closest to him. And to back up that claim—to be able to report *anything* significant to constituents—a lawmaker would have to negotiate creative deals with lawmakers from other camps. The most skillful negotiators would, in fact, have the most progress to report to their own voters and would therefore have the highest odds of winning reelection.

This scenario, optimistic as it sounds, is exactly how most negotiations we've witnessed have played out: Representatives for the various sides realized that to make any progress for their own causes they had to negotiate with one another. Each one then sold the deal to his or her own side.

Even so, whenever we suggest that Congress could work this way, we get barraged with questions. We promise to answer them in this book. For now, we want to briefly respond to two doubts. First, our proposed changes are entirely consistent with the Constitution. In fact, as you will see, America's founders wanted to create the kind of bond between lawmakers and their constituents that our changes would create.

Second, we realize that many voters don't fit neatly into a political category: liberal, conservative, *or* moderate. So, in the elections we'll propose, voters would not have to choose a category. Each voter would in fact be freer than ever to define him- or herself politically.

Still, many people will wonder whether such dramatic changes are possible. We will answer those doubts too. You will see that by a series of modest steps our elections can be overhauled, with the end result that Congress would resolve major national problems sensibly. To make that case, we just need to lay out the key pieces of the puzzle in the right order.

To start, in part I, you will see what it would take for our country to develop practical solutions to nearly every major issue, solutions that all sides would support. We'll put you in the same room with liberals and conservatives, environmentalists and industrialists, moguls and labor union leaders who have hammered out unanimous agreements on some of today's most contentious issues, including how to slash our consumption of foreign oil, how to repair Social Security, and how to preserve the environment at the least cost to everyone. In each case, you'll see exactly why fierce advocates worked so hard to strike constructive agreements with their long-standing enemies.

In part II, you'll see exactly why our elected politicians so rarely do the same. You'll witness a concerned citizen win a seat in Congress, determined with all his heart to do the job well. But *two* basic features of our elections undermine all his efforts, virtually compelling him to fight over problems rather than resolve them. And with every lawmaker mired in that predicament, Congress consistently mismanages the major challenges of our time.

In part III, you'll see how we, the American people, can turn our bickering lawmakers into the kind of problem-solvers you met in part I. You'll see that we can restructure our elections so that the lawmakers who negotiate genuine solutions to our nation's troubles will win reelection, while those who just posture and bicker will be weeded out.

If you still doubt that our politicians will ever tackle our major problems sensibly, just keep in mind that politicians are flesh and blood. They're human beings like the rest of us. They respond to rewards and incentives like the rest of us. We just need elections that will give our politicians the right incentives. Then, at last, they will start to craft genuine solutions.

Part I:
Politics at Its Best

1

How Do Outsiders Solve Problems
That Politicians Won't?

D avid Buzzelli wasn't especially fond of Washington, D.C., which he
visited often for his job as vice president of environmental affairs at
Dow Chemical. But on that July day in 1993, the nation's capital was
where Buzzelli wanted to be. As for the others in the wood-paneled conference
room, most of them looked uncomfortable. The CEOs of Chevron Oil, Pacific
Gas & Electric, S. C. Johnson, Ciba-Geigy, and Georgia-Pacific fidgeted in their
seats, some with their jaws clenched. Staring back at them were leaders of the
Sierra Club, the Environmental Defense Fund, and the Natural Resources Defense Council. Interspersed among these long-standing enemies were the head
of the Environmental Protection Agency (EPA) and the secretaries of interior,
commerce, and energy. Buzzelli expected the session to become volatile. He
had often heard the environmentalists accuse the CEOs of poisoning the country's air, land, and water. The CEOs had, in turn, often accused the environmentalists of sabotaging American prosperity by demanding regulations that
were costing industry hundreds of billions of dollars to comply with. Many at
the table were suing each other.

Yet, Buzzelli mused, they're all here, sitting down face-to-face—mostly out
of frustration with their endless combat. Businesses and environmental groups
had by that time collectively spent a billion man-hours battling each other, only
to reach a standoff, with each side realizing that it would never vanquish the
other. The corporate executives knew that Americans would forever demand a
cleaner environment. The environmentalists knew that Americans would keep
demanding the jobs and products that industry provided.

Even so, coaxing all of these people to meet face-to-face had required an invitation from the president of the United States. He or his emissaries had urged each one to attend this meeting, saying more or less, "By talking directly with your adversaries, perhaps you can work out a long-term solution that all of you can live with." In that spirit, President Bill Clinton planned to call the group his Council on Sustainable Development (CSD).

To cochair the council, the president had picked Buzzelli and Jonathan Lash, an environmentalist who headed the World Resources Institute. Both men were known for advocating cooperation with the other's camp.

Both men realized, though, that long-standing enemies didn't make peace easily. They were quickly proved right. At the first two council meetings, the members continued to vent hostility and suspicion. But no one from either camp wanted to keep spending time and money on warfare. So, they all agreed to keep meeting.

During the next few sessions, Buzzelli and Lash coaxed each council member to acknowledge that his or her opponents had legitimate concerns. The business executives admitted that pollution harmed everyone's quality of life, including their own and that of their employees and stockholders. So a cleaner environment would benefit businesses as much as any group. Besides, companies didn't *want* to produce pollution. It was a by-product that they would gladly be rid of.

As for the environmental members of the council, they acknowledged that nearly every American depended on the products, services, jobs, and pay that businesses provided. A thriving economy was therefore in everyone's interests. The environmentalists also conceded that the regulations to control pollution often required companies to use technologies that quickly became outdated. Innovators were constantly developing more efficient, less costly methods.

By sharing these realities with one another, all twenty-five council members were able to agree on a common objective. They vowed to find ways to clean up the environment at the least cost to everyone.

To get there, the council members spent two years gathering data, seeking input from hundreds of outside experts, and brainstorming among themselves. The various camps then engaged in some hard negotiating.

By February 1996, all twenty-five members had agreed on how to make major progress on the key environmental questions of that time. They spelled out the details in a 185-page report.

Its main theme was a "grand bargain." The council proposed that the government require industries to clean up the environment more thoroughly than they had to date, but without detailed regulations. Instead, companies would largely decide *how* to comply with the tougher standards. Businesses could then use their ingenuity to find the most effective and efficient ways to cut pollution.

To back up this plan, the CSD cited cases when the EPA had given companies similar latitude in how they met environmental benchmarks. Each time, the EPA got a cleaner environment than it would have by traditional means, while the businesses saved money. The CSD projected that if this approach were applied nationwide, industry could in time save hundreds of billions of dollars. Businesses could thus lower their prices, thereby benefiting consumers. Everyone would win.

As soon as the CSD issued its report, the members fanned out across the country to pitch their plan to their allies in the outside world. Buzzelli, for instance, showed the members of the Chemical Manufacturers Association how the CSD's plan would serve their interests. Meanwhile, Georgia-Pacific CEO Peter Correll presented the whole package to wood and paper industry executives whom he had known for years. Jonathan Lash spoke with many people on the other side of the fence, to environmental leaders who knew him as a colleague and ally. As a result, nearly every major environmental group ended up endorsing the council's blueprint. So did the relevant industry associations, labor unions, and government agencies.

Buzzelli, Lash, and the other council members felt pride in a job well done. Each one also hoped that, for his or her own camp, a better future lay ahead.

Those hopes soon began to crumble, though. If the CSD's vision of a pristine environment coupled with greater prosperity was to become reality, Congress had to act. Yet most lawmakers ignored the CSD's plan. Republicans kept trying to gut environmental laws, while Democrats repeatedly blocked efforts to reduce regulations. In nearly every election campaign since then, Democrats have bashed polluters, while Republicans have bashed environmentalists.

The environment is apparently too good a campaign issue to lose to a mere solution.

Other Americans who creatively solved major national problems have suffered the same fate. In early 1997, for instance, twenty-four industry executives, academics, and government officials from across the ideological spectrum met to save Social Security from eventual collapse. Gathering in Washington, D.C., they vowed to find ways that future generations could retire with some financial security—without bankrupting the U.S. Treasury. The group called itself the National Commission on Retirement Policy. The members knew that any change in Social Security could stir controversy. Cutting benefits would anger the voters who would lose them, while raising Social Security taxes would anger the voters who would have to pay them. Congress, afraid to take either approach, had been paralyzed for years.

Yet, after deliberating for eighteen months, all twenty-four commission members agreed on how to best meet everyone's needs. They proposed that the government (a) give workers tax incentives to save more toward retirement, (b) give businesses tax incentives to create retirement programs for all of their workers, (c) guarantee the neediest citizens a minimum Social Security benefit, and (d) pay for all of the above by slowly raising the age at which people could receive full Social Security benefits.

Although every commission member supported these conclusions and experts across the spectrum backed similar plans, most lawmakers refused to support any reform. Most Democrats kept silent even after President Clinton backed some features of the commission's plan. And years later most Republicans kept silent even after President George W. Bush made Social Security reform his top domestic priority. The chair of the Senate Finance Committee admitted that most of his colleagues wished the issue would just "go away." Congressional leaders have been so terrified of modifying Social Security that to this date they have refused even to schedule debates on the subject. The typical legislator would apparently prefer that Social Security ruin this country's finances rather than risk his or her seat.

Congress has ducked other critical issues that outsiders have shown precisely how to solve. In December 2004, sixteen corporate CEOs, environmental leaders, academics, and former government officials agreed unanimously on how America could best meet its ravenous need for energy. The group, called the National Commission on Energy Policy (NCEP), issued a 148-page report on how to cut our consumption of oil, reduce foreign imports, and slow down global warming, all at a minimal cost.

The commission proposed limiting the amount of climate-changing gases that businesses would be allowed to produce, while also letting companies sell allocations they didn't need to companies that did need them. For years, utilities had used that kind of trading system to control pollutants at lower cost than other types of regulation.

The commission proposed extending that concept to the automobile industry, by requiring car companies to sharply increase gasoline mileage, while also letting them trade mileage credits with one another. For instance, if cars were required to average forty miles per gallon, one company could produce cars averaging thirty-five miles per gallon if another agreed to produce the same number averaging forty-five miles per gallon.

The commission also urged building plants to convert America's huge supply of coal, the most polluting carbon fuel, into the equivalent of natural gas, one of the least polluting fuels.

Regarding politicians' favorite energy policy—subsidizing ethanol made from corn—the commission raised several doubts, saying that approach would cost more, yield more pollution, and use more energy than burning gasoline alone.

How did Congress respond to this detailed plan for obtaining energy without harm to the economy or the environment? By ignoring it. The 2005 energy bill consisted mostly of tax breaks for oil and gas companies, which will likely *increase* our consumption of oil and speed up global warming. Congress also continued to encourage wider use of ethanol, which has benefited corn farmers but not the nation's energy policy. And in late 2007, when Congress did mandate a 2 percent annual increase in gas mileage over the next thirteen years, the NCEP estimated that step would reduce America's greenhouse gases emissions by just 4 percent.

Ideological adversaries who were not elected officials have even outdone politicians on emotionally charged issues such as abortion. In Buffalo, Denver, St. Louis, and Washington D.C., a group called the Common Ground Network for Life and Choice has brought advocates for all sides to the same table. Although the network's leaders were mainly trying to promote dialogue, in several cities the opponents continued meeting until they agreed on ways to reduce the number of abortions. In Buffalo, the various sides worked out a program to discourage teenagers from getting pregnant. In St. Louis, the opposing camps developed a program to help couples adopt newborn infants.

Meanwhile, most lawmakers refuse to sit down with their opponents to discuss the issue of abortion.

Congress itself has admitted that political adversaries outside the government can solve problems that officials inside the government cannot. Under the Negotiated Rulemaking Act of 1990, Congress gave opposing interest groups the right to draft certain federal regulations. When a federal agency tackles a particularly controversial issue, for instance, the agency may fear that any proposal it comes up with will anger some interest groups—enough so that they will file lawsuits to block the plan. To avoid that kind of fight, the agency can invite every relevant interest group to send a spokesperson to Washington. If all of those representatives can agree on a regulation, the agency can adopt it, confident that all the concerned parties will support the decision.

Long-standing opponents have used this procedure to negotiate regulations about nuclear wastes, food inspections, student loans, public housing, and Medicare payments. In every case, all parties endorsed the outcome.

There are thousands of similar stories (some of them in appendix I). In every case, politicians were stymied—unwilling or unable to reconcile their differences. Yet representatives from outside the government tackled the same issue and negotiated a practical solution that every side accepted.

What is it about these ideological adversaries that enabled them to solve problems that politicians wouldn't?

In most cases, each successful negotiator had a large group of people counting on him or her personally to advance a cause they all shared and cared about passionately. Take the Council on Sustainable Development. Each environmental leader spoke for dozens of colleagues and thousands of contributors to their organizations, all intent on protecting the environment. Meanwhile, each corporate CEO spoke for thousands of other executives, all intent on boosting their companies' performance. Each representative thereby felt unrelenting pressure to advance his or her own camp's agenda.

Each spokesperson realized, though, that to make real progress for his or her own camp, he or she had to strike a deal with long-standing opponents. Each representative was then ideally positioned to explain to all the people in his or her camp—in terms compelling to them—how that deal with their long-time enemies would advance their own cause.

By the same process, could our nation develop genuine solutions to our other pressing issues: health care, national security, public education, taxes, whatever? For all the issues that matter, could we find realistic solutions that Americans of all persuasions would welcome—just by bringing together the right representatives with the right motivation?

2

How to Resolve Any Issue—as Well as Humanly Possible

For every controversy dividing our country, there are representatives who have the knowledge, the tenacity, and the standing to find practical solutions—and then to win support for those solutions from Americans of all stripes. As you might expect, many people find that claim hard to believe, given the bitter tone of politics in these times. But we have found that there are ways to persuade even the most skeptical Americans that our country could find genuine solutions to even the most divisive issues. One such conversation with a lifelong political activist—a liberal, it turned out—went essentially like this:

"I've fought with conservatives over tax reform since my twenties. And every change that I pushed for drove those conservatives nuts. It was as if they came from another planet. Their values were the opposite of mine. We will never agree on how to structure taxes."

"As a mediator, I've seen the fiercest of adversaries negotiate agreements—even on issues as contentious as how to satisfy America's need for energy, how to slow down global warming, how to . . . "

"That doesn't convince me that opposing camps could resolve *any* issue."

"But if opposing camps combine their ingenuity, doesn't it make sense that they can get a better result than if they devote their ingenuity to undercutting one another?"

"If their interests directly clash, I don't see how they have any basis for an agreement."

"Okay. I can show you that opponents, no matter how far apart, can find a practical solution to any controversy—if they put their minds to it. But to make that case, I need to start with a conflict that's less complicated than your thirty-year battle with conservatives."

"Like what?"

"Any conflict that matters to you, perhaps something from your own life."

"How about a battle I'm having at home?"

"Sure. That'll do for a first example."

"Okay. My wife and I are fighting over where our daughter Leslie will go to college."

"I've witnessed plenty of families go through that. How is it affecting you?"

"As I see it, Leslie should go to our state university. It's a good school, and we can afford it. Going to a state school didn't do me any harm."

"How does your wife feel about it?"

"She sneers at our state university. She wants Leslie to go to Columbia, the highest-rated school that her guidance counselor says she can get into. I'd like to send her, but we're mortgaged up to our eyeballs. We don't have the cash. Yet my wife and I earn too much for Leslie to get financial aid. As for student loans, Leslie doesn't want to bury herself in debt like her folks."

"Okay. Have you considered other schools?"

"Yeah, but we can't seem to agree on any."

"What about Leslie? Where does she want to go?"

"She's been okay with about half of the colleges we've looked at so far. She mainly wants my wife and me to make peace."

"You can. You'll see. To start, I'd need you to rate all the colleges that you or your wife have considered and that Leslie would accept—say on a scale from zero to ten."

"Sure. I could do that."

"Then, I'd need your wife to rate all the schools."

"Okay. I expect she'd play along."

"Next, we'd need to put all those ratings on a chart."

"I hate those kinds of charts."

"What if this chart can help solve *any* conflict you care about?"

"All right. Let's see it."

"The chart would start out looking like this:"

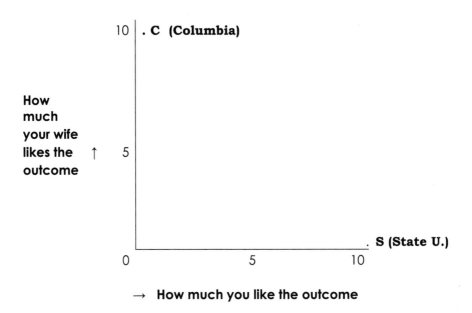

"What am I looking at?"

"On this grid, your state university is labeled with the letter *S*. I gather you'd rate it a ten."

"Given our situation, yes."

"But if I'm hearing you right, your wife would give it a zero."

"Or an even a lower number, if you'd let her."

"Meanwhile, Columbia is labeled *C*. I assume that would be your wife's ten."

"You got that right."

"For you, though, I'm guessing it's dead last."

"Reluctantly."

"Okay. Name another college you've considered and how you'd rate it."

"The University of Wisconsin. It beats our state school academically. But to out-of-staters like us, it's also more expensive. And the travel would cost a lot more. So I'd give it a five."

"And your wife?"

"Good as Wisconsin is, it isn't Ivy League. My guess is she'd give it a four."

"So, we could add Wisconsin to the chart this way:"

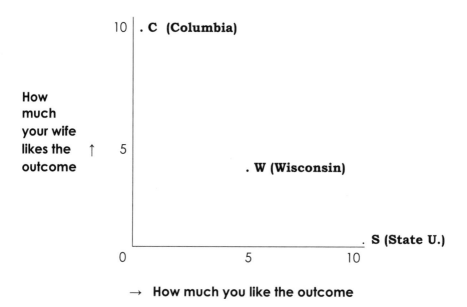

"I get the idea. It's not exactly rocket science."

"Agreed. So we could easily add all the other schools that you and your wife have thought about."

"And I should care?"

"Well, when all the schools were on the grid, it might end up looking something like this: "

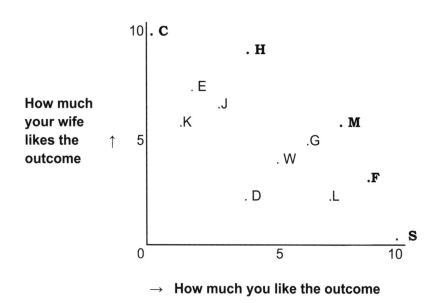

→ **How much you like the outcome**

"What's the big deal?"

"The beauty of this chart is that the best outcomes end up on the right-hand boundary. In this case, those points are C, H, M, F, and S. They beat all the alternatives."

"What do you mean they beat all the alternatives?"

"Well, pick any point that isn't on that boundary."

"It looks like my top pick among the other choices would be L."

"Yes, but notice that you'd prefer F over L."

"I can see that."

"Your wife would prefer F over L, too."

"Yeah, I see. So what?"

"If you pick *any* point off the boundary, you can find some point *on* it that's better for *both* sides."

"Wait. I see that for both of us, M beats G, W, and D."

"And for both of you, H beats the three remaining points."

"Got it. I see that the boundary points are the best outcomes."

"That's why the boundary is called the 'efficient frontier.'"

"Nice concept. It still doesn't solve my problem. This so-called frontier has five points. How do we decide on one? My wife insists on Columbia. No way that's going to happen. We'd end up in the poorhouse."

"I get it. Likewise, when you push for your state university, your wife won't budge. So what if you considered the midpoint of the frontier, whatever school is represented by M? Of the five frontier points, it's the one that's fairest to both of you."

"Sounds good in theory, but my wife and I haven't even come close to agreeing."

"Because in the heat of battle, each of you has pushed your own point of view. You've mainly advocated outcomes that favored your own concerns."

"That's more or less true."

"Imagine, though, if you thought of new, more creative ways to get Leslie a quality education. If you put all those outcomes on the chart, it would have a new boundary, a few points better than all the others. The midpoint of *that* frontier would be better than anything you've considered so far."

"That's easy to say. But how would we find these 'more creative,' more promising possibilities?"

"Focus on what your real 'interests' are in this situation."

"What do you mean?"

"You want Leslie to get a good education at a price you can afford, right?"

"Yeah."

"So do you and your wife spend money on things you'd both be willing to cut back on?"

"We go on vacations to some pretty remote places. My wife gets a big kick out of them, but she cares even more about Leslie's future. As do I."

"So if you forgo those trips for a few years, you could afford to send Leslie someplace more expensive than your state university."

"Yes. But we still couldn't afford Columbia, which my wife would still insist on."

"So let's deal with her concerns. Why, exactly, is your wife set on Columbia?"

"She says an Ivy League degree will give Leslie the best shot at a great job after college."

"It would probably help, but it's not the only way for her to get a good start. What if Leslie worked at a first-class firm during her summer vacations? Wouldn't that stand out on her résumé even more than an Ivy League degree?"

"Sure. Recruiters care more about real experience than just a sheepskin."

"So can you help Leslie get a high-profile internship?"

"I know some honchos at the big-name consulting firms. I could get at least one of them to meet with Leslie. And anyone who did would pick up on how bright she is. I'd bet he'd hire her. Then, she'd wow him. She's a great kid. She'd get amazing evaluations."

"Perfect. So if you help Leslie line up that kind of internship for this summer, you'd build up her résumé even more than a top college might. Wouldn't that meet your wife's main concern?"

"It should. What a relief that would be."

"So do you see how this situation relates to your battles with conservatives?"

"Not really."

"The main connection is this: people often wind up far apart because each one clings to a specific 'position' without looking for other possibilities. You and your wife, for instance, are stuck because you're attached to specific schools. To find a solution, you'll have to put aside the specific outcome—for a while—and instead think about your real 'interests,' your main needs and wants. In this case, you're determined to live within your means while your wife is focusing on Leslie's career. As you've seen, you can meet both needs. And if you spend more time on it, you'll think up plenty more ways to do so. Likewise, political opponents usually have many more ways to satisfy their needs than they've considered. And they are guaranteed to find more of those ways if they work together than if they fight."

"Hold on. My wife and I will work things out because we both want what's best for Leslie. We both want to maintain peace in our family. But how do real enemies find a solution that all sides can accept?"

"In *any* situation, there's an efficient frontier. In any conflict, there are deals that will benefit all sides as much as humanly possible—which they can find only if they combine their ingenuity and resources."

"But political opponents usually have diametrically opposing interests."

"Much less often than most people think. Give me an example of what you see as directly clashing interests."

"Well, suppose two nations draw most of their drinking water from the same river. So they fight constantly over who gets how much. One side's gain would be the other's loss."

"Don't both countries have a mutual interest in keeping the water pure and making it last? Don't both want to find new supplies? Don't they both depend on other natural resources that they could develop together?"

"I imagine. But *some* political adversaries have directly opposing interests."

"Some people *think* so—that other cultures, religions, or ethnic groups have interests or values diametrically opposed to their own. That's why ethnic and religious conflicts can be so tough to resolve. The parties often want to annihilate each other."

"I can name conservatives who want to annihilate liberal organizations I belong to. I feel the same about some right-wing groups. Our goals clash head-on. Our interests directly clash."

"That's how it appears. But name an issue where you think your interests are at odds."

"I believe in helping the poor. Conservatives don't."

"Do conservatives want to keep people in poverty?"

"They don't want to do anything about it."

"Isn't it more accurate to say that most people on the right want to reduce poverty but differ with you about the best ways to do it? After all, it was a conservative economist, Milton Friedman, who proposed the negative income tax, paying cash directly to those below the poverty line."

"Oh yeah, I remember that one. All right, I'll accept that conservatives would reduce poverty—if they could dismantle nearly every government program aimed at reducing it."

"The way they put it is that they want to eliminate bureaucracy. The truth is that both liberals and conservatives want to reduce poverty, but they disagree about what works."

"Maybe in that case. But look at where the right wing stands on taxes. They want to eliminate the inheritance tax, capital gains taxes, and corporate taxes. Anything to help the rich."

"The way conservatives frame it is that they want every person or company to reap the fruits of their own success, not be punished with extra taxes."

"Whatever. I still say that the left and right have directly opposing interests on that issue."

"Don't liberals and conservatives agree that the current tax code is impossible to comprehend, is unfair, and is a drain on the economy? Don't both sides want a simpler tax system? Don't both sides want a tax code that promotes economic growth? Don't left and right both want a tax system that all sides consider fair?"

"In principle, perhaps. But we could never agree on the details."

"You could never agree if you *started* with the details."

"So, where would we start?"

"First off, you would need the right representatives."

"What does that mean?"

"Let me give you the classic example. Remember when South Africa repealed apartheid?"

"Sure. In the early 1990s. It happened so quickly—after years of bloody stalemate."

"What made it happen were the two negotiators: F. W. de Klerk and Nelson Mandela, South Africa's white supremacist prime minister meeting face-to-face with the hero of most black South Africans. Both men knew that if they struck a deal that made sense to them, each one could sell it to his own camp. Which they did. De Klerk persuaded most whites that they had to make peace with the ever more militant black majority. Meanwhile, Mandela convinced most blacks that to gain equality they had to guarantee the then-entrenched white minority some power in future governments. Who else could have negotiated a deal that nearly every South African would abide by?"

"I see your point about choosing the right representatives."

"It's pretty straightforward. To resolve a tough political conflict, each camp has to have a representative it trusts. Because to accept that a deal with their long-standing enemies is truly fair, people have to believe that their representative is on their side. They have to believe that he or she truly has their interests at heart."

"Makes sense. So how would that principle apply to fixing the U.S. Tax Code?"

"We'd need to assemble a small group of representatives—maybe fifteen—each of whom had lots of credibility on the subject of taxes. We'd need to pick them in such a way that just about every American who felt strongly about the issue could point to one of the fifteen and say: 'I trust that person on the subject of taxes. If she backed major changes in the tax code, I'd certainly listen to her make her case.'"

"Assembling a group like that sounds like an impossibly tall order."

"On any issue, there's a handful of people who have the highest public profile. To find the most efficient ways to clean up the environment, for instance, the Clinton administration enlisted the heads of major environmental groups, the CEOs of six top corporations, and so on."

"I get the idea. On taxes, who would I trust? Maybe Clinton's first secretary of labor, Robert Reich, a savvy economist whose politics I like very much. My centrist friends might pick Robert Rubin, whom they say was the best treasury secretary of the last century. What about conservatives? The ones I know might opt for Bush's last treasury secretary, Hank Paulson."

"Good choices. Plus it would help to include a well-known labor union leader, a prominent corporate CEO, and tax experts from think tanks such as the Brookings Institution, the Heritage Foundation, the Progressive Policy Institute, and so on."

"Okay, I can see how the people we've named could sell an agreement to most Americans. But given that they would have such different ideologies and agendas, I don't see how they could reach agreement on an issue as divisive as taxes."

"You just admitted that all sides could agree on general objectives: a fairer, simpler, more economically efficient tax code."

"But that's not enough for them to strike a deal."

"It's nowhere near enough. But it is the first step. Next, they'd have to explore alternative ways to structure the tax system and evaluate how each alternative would advance or hinder their broad objectives."

"You must be kidding. The possibilities are endless. And each option would have more effects than anyone could predict."

"True. But if the people we've named put their minds to it, don't you think they could come up with more promising alternatives than any camp could on its own? Just consider all the mental energy that liberal and conservative advocates have spent hammering each other on the subject of taxes. Imagine if some of that brain power was put to work looking for the most productive ways to achieve what all sides want."

"If Reich, Rubin, Paulson, and the rest of them were really committed to it, I suppose they could dream up some good ideas. But each of them would *still* want a different tax structure."

"Yes. So each one would have to focus on his or her top priority. They would then need to trade, as in 'I'll accept this proposal that you want most, if you give me that one that I want most.' With those trades, they could put together a package that all of them could accept."

"It can't be that easy."

"I didn't say it would be easy. I just say that they could do it. I've told you about all the political foes I've seen negotiate creative agreements on some very tough issues."

"But taxes are a far more convoluted subject than most. In any deal on taxes, some groups would lose out."

"Not if it were done right. A saner tax code would save hundreds of billions of dollars a year. Nearly every economist says so. And with that much savings, there must be ways to divvy up the benefits so that just about everyone would come out ahead of where they are now."

"In theory, perhaps. But you'd never convince everyone that they'd gotten a fair shake."

"True. There are always some people who feel dissatisfied, some people who feel they should have done better, some people who are sure that they know the one right way to handle an issue and won't budge from that position. So in any political battle, the best that negotiators can do is to win over the vast majority of people in each camp. But that is doable."

"The current tax code is such a mess that I can accept that there must be ways to make it simpler, economically saner, and fairer for just about everyone. But none of that guarantees it will happen. There must be many ways to screw up any negotiation."

"A few. For one thing, every negotiator is pulled in two directions. Each one wants the most benefits for his or her own side. Yet each one also wants the *other* parties to contribute their best ideas toward a solution. And to make that happen, a negotiator has to cooperate with his supposed enemies. Nearly every representative struggles to find the right balance between cooperating with his opponents and grabbing all he can for his own camp."

"How does anyone know what constitutes the 'right balance'?"

"There's no magic formula. So it's a good idea for a neutral facilitator to run all the meetings. He or she can then coax anyone who gets too demanding."

"Say, that works. You're sure that this council of fifteen would strike a deal?"

"No. But I am sure that negotiation is every camp's best option. I am sure that to get the fairest, most productive tax code, all sides would have to work together. What do you think would work better? Your side's current tactics? If you stick to them, when do you expect to see a tax code that serves America's best interests as you see them?"

"Not in my lifetime."

"So, would you favor this kind of negotiation, with all sides trying to hash things out face-to-face?"

"Sure, why not? It sounds more promising than what my liberal friends and I are doing now."

In roughly the same way, we've shown Americans elsewhere on the spectrum that opposing camps can find practical solutions to almost any issue—solutions that all sides would welcome. Finding those solutions just requires assembling the right representatives with the right motivation.

There's just one problem. For any solution to become law, Congress would have to enact it. But as things now stand, Congress is a black hole into which first-rate solutions disappear, never to see the light of day. Just look at how Congress has ignored proposals from the Council on Sustainable Development, the National Commission on Energy Policy, and so on.

How, then, can America resolve the many controversial issues that threaten to tear our country apart? We will have to motivate our politicians to negotiate genuine solution to those issues.

Fortunately, history offers hints about how to do just that.

3

Could Politicians Negotiate the Best Solutions?

Amerca has at times faced even more serious problems than it does today, and our politicians have often risen to the challenge—eventually. The most dramatic example occurred when our nation was struggling to be born. The year was 1787. Our national government existed on paper, but it had almost no power over the states or their citizens. Each state even issued its own currency, which made trade among the states so cumbersome that our economy grew only sporadically. Some areas were sliding toward a depression. The states also lacked a joint military and a coherent foreign policy. Several European countries expected the American federation to collapse, at which point they intended to plunder the New World again. Many prominent Americans feared that fate might indeed await them. So they lobbied their states to organize a convention to find ways of strengthening their union. Twelve states chose to participate. Each one picked some leading citizens as delegates.

As soon as the delegates met in Philadelphia, though, they formed opposing camps. Benjamin Franklin observed that he and his fellow delegates had brought to the convention "all their prejudices, their passions, their errors of opinion, their local interests, and their selfish views."

They certainly did. Selfish local interests collided just about every day of that convention. Delegates from the most populous states demanded seats in a new Congress in proportion to their population. The smaller states refused, insisting that each state have an equal voice. Delegates from the North wanted to limit slavery. Southern-state delegates threatened to walk out. States abutting virgin land in the West claimed it as their own. States without access to the western frontier objected. Delegates from the richest states feared the poorer states were after their wealth. The poorest states feared the richest ones would dominate them. The southern states, which exported a great deal of produce, wanted free trade. Northern states wanted to tax those exports.

The delegates also clashed over ideology, as much as Congress feuds today, and over many of the same principles. The delegates fought over how much power to give the federal government over the states. They differed on how much political clout ordinary citizens should have compared to the rich. They disagreed over who should have more leverage: Congress or the president. Sound familiar?

Each delegate realized, though, that if he went home without an agreement, his own state would suffer economically and remain vulnerable to foreign invaders. So, despite that summer's sweltering heat, the delegates negotiated for four months in a small room sealed off from public view.

Each delegate, to make maximum progress on the issues most critical to his state, gave ground on other issues. To put together an agreement that every state could accept, each delegate had to give up some of his wish list. No one saw the final document, the Constitution, as perfect.

But nearly every delegate went along with Ben Franklin's assessment that it was the best solution possible at that time. Of the fifty-five men who met in Philadelphia, all but six supported the final result.

They then had to persuade their states to ratify the Constitution, which proved as hard as creating the document itself. After all, the framers had had a unique experience. They had bargained for four months over every major issue confronting the states at the time. They had weighed how each option might play out. They had evaluated many possible combinations of options. After all that back-and-forth, the framers saw their disagreements in a different light than they had at first.

To show the public what they had discovered and to win support for the Constitution, the delegates had to wage a campaign tailored to each state. Each state had its own social conditions, its own economy, its own priorities. Massachusetts fishermen, for instance, lived different lives than South Carolina cotton planters. Persuading all thirteen states to sign up for the new republic took the framers and their allies three years.

How big was their achievement? Was the Constitution the best solution to America's difficulties that men of that time could have achieved? It certainly wasn't perfect. The Constitution allowed slavery. It let the states disenfranchise women and the poor. But that's how the world worked in the 1780s. Kings and nobles ruled nearly every country. Given those conditions, could we have done any better? The Constitution surely moved us a long way toward its stated goals: "to form a more perfect union, establish justice, insure domestic tranquility, provide for the common defense, promote the general welfare, and secure the blessings of liberty."

Fifty-five representatives made that success possible. One group of people meeting in one room.

If they could find the most practical solutions to the pressing issues of their time, why can't Congress do as good a job of managing our current problems? Nearly every citizen and commentator blames Washington's deadlocks on partisanship or the power of interest groups. A few pundits also condemn various blocs of voters for making unreasonable demands.

But these so-called explanations explain almost nothing. After all, competing ideas, strong interest groups, and demanding citizens are what make our democracy work. Just look at how we acquired our Constitution. Each of the framers fought for the most powerful interests in his home state. The founders also waged fierce ideological battles. Plus each one struggled to appease citizens back home. And all of these steps were necessary to resolve the differences among the thirteen states and unite them into one nation.

Politics today is much the same. Assertive partisans, vocal interest groups, and demanding citizens often play key roles in resolving major national problems. Just look at the Council on Sustainable Development, the National Commission on Retirement Policy, or the Commission on Energy Policy. Ideological adversaries of all kinds struck creative bargains—because each one knew that to make lasting progress for his or her own cause, he had to negotiate with the other camps.

Lawmakers are in the same position. If they genuinely wanted to advance the causes they claim to stand for, they too would negotiate enduring agreements with their opponents. Instead, our lawmakers battle over today's problems, leaving them largely unresolved. Partisanship cannot explain that phenomenon. True partisans want to implement their agenda and see it endure, not just posture and bicker.

Something besides partisanship is driving our lawmakers. And until we, the American people, understand exactly what it is, we will be stuck with the politics of perpetual combat, a politics that most of us have come to hate.

Fortunately, there is a compelling explanation for why our politicians behave so perversely.

Part II: Why Our Lawmakers Betray Us

W. Edwards Deming, once the world's top expert on quality control, often said that if *most* people filling a particular job are performing it badly, something must be wrong with that *job*. That insight applies to politicians as much as anyone. After all, nearly every lawmaker fights over national problems more than solves them—which strongly suggests that the job of lawmaker is fatally flawed.

Why, then, haven't you heard about the defects? There is so much information available about politicians that even the experts seem unable to piece it all together. Just look at how the CIA and FBI gathered reams of information about terrorism before September 11, 2001. Yet both agencies failed to weave those facts into a clear picture of what the terrorists were up to. Both agencies, according to the 9/11 Commission, had failed "to connect the dots."

Likewise, America's pundits and journalists have failed to provide a credible explanation for why nearly every lawmaker fights endlessly over the major issues. The pundits may have too much data or be too close to their subject to see the big picture.

As for politicians themselves, most don't want to reveal what truly drives their actions. To some extent, they may not even know.

In our years as mediators, though, we've discovered things about politicians' motives that few people have any opportunity to observe. By refereeing many conflicts, we've discerned why politicians battle incessantly with one another. To show you what we have seen, we need to weave many facts and events of the past few years into one coherent picture.

The most effective way we've found to connect all those dots is to tell you the story of one concerned citizen so troubled about the state of American politics that he decides to run for Congress. When he wins the seat, he then has to deal with his constituents, staff, and fellow lawmakers, which proves to be a far harder job than he had expected.

To show you the many pressures that politicians face, the characters in the following chapters are composites of real people. Their dialogue, though imagined, explains more about what drives lawmakers today than anything else we've seen.

And understanding what truly drives our lawmakers is the only way we can all start to repair our country's broken political process.

4

Each Lawmaker's Predicament: Whom Do I Represent?

Tom Hennessey was widely respected in his suburban community for having taken over the failing local high school and, within a decade, turning it into a showcase that was earning a statewide reputation for excellence. Tom's frequent op-eds in regional newspapers, faulting Washington politicians for how they handled public education, further enhanced his standing. So when the local member of Congress, Roger Blake, developed heart trouble and retired in mid-term, many friends encouraged Tom to run for the seat. His next-door neighbor, Paul Jaffe, said, "Now you have a chance to act on your convictions."

Tom was torn over what to do. He loved being a high school principal, both helping adolescents in trouble and helping the best and brightest fulfill their potential. Some of his students had written to Tom over the years to thank him and tell him of their successes, occasionally including pictures of their wives and children. Tom often recalled those letters at times when the job began to drain him.

At the same time, Tom was growing increasingly angry over what he saw as the federal government's incompetence. He'd even had a run-in with a senator that had left him muttering, "What drives these people?" Now, he had an opportunity to act on his anger.

Tom wondered how his wife Kelley would react to what he was contemplating. Having met as young teachers, they had been married for twenty-six years. They had two children, Janet and Ryan. After they were born, Kelley had switched careers. She had capitalized on her skills with languages by starting a business translating legal documents and business materials. She did some of the work herself and recruited part-timers over the Internet. Some years, Kelley made more money than Tom did.

"Much as I love my job," Tom tells his wife, "I feel in my gut that I'm supposed to go for this. I want to leave more of a legacy than I will as a principal."

"I don't want to hold you back, sweetheart. But I would hate being apart most of the time."

"I would too. But with Janet away at college and Ryan headed there next year, you could soon spend some weeks in D.C. with me, couldn't you?"

"Let me sleep on it," Kelley responds.

The following morning, seeing the hunger in Tom's eyes for this challenge, Kelley reluctantly gives her blessing. "I can feel how much you want this."

"It's worth doing," he says. "You'll see."

Tom starts by meeting with local power brokers to spell out how he would represent the district. Most of them approve of his plans. Some offer to write a check. Though Tom feels awkward taking the money, at first, he accepts it and opens a campaign account. Many people he speaks to spread the word about him.

Encouraged by the support, Tom puts his heart into the campaign. Running the school by day, he travels around the district at night to speak with local civic groups. Most people like what they see. Tom is six feet tall, graying at the temples, and lean, with a slight scar on his jaw from his college days as a boxer. His voice is also an asset, conveying both sincerity and passion, enough so that Tom overshadows the two other candidates from his party. He wins the primary easily.

Campaigning even harder for the general election, Tom neglects his job, his wife, and his children, but promises to make it up to them. On the day of the special election in late January, it's cold and wet. Tom worries that the freezing rain will discourage all but the most civic minded from going to the polls. Only 8 percent of eligible voters show up to vote.

But Tom's reputation, on top of his coming from the same party as the retiring incumbent, helps him win by a comfortable margin. Hearing the result at his campaign headquarters with his strongest supporters congratulating him, Tom feels exhilarated.

Yet over the next few days, as he ties up loose ends, Tom feels anxious about the dramatic life change in front of him. Three days after the election, with a knot in his gut, he kisses his wife good-bye at the airport. On the plane to Washington, Tom tries to read but can't.

His mind drifts back to an incident from his Peace Corps days teaching English in an African village. One night Tom came upon a local bully forcing himself on a frightened young girl. When Tom intervened and the bully came at him with a knife, Tom came close to killing the man. Though the local authorities concluded that Tom had acted in self-defense, ever since he has not spoken of this event, not to a priest, not to friends, not even to his wife. He has kept the memory of his rage at a distance—as he used to blot out pain in the boxing ring, so he could finish the match. Tom wonders why this memory is intruding on him now. As the plane nears Washington, he wonders if anything could provoke that kind of rage in him again.

The following morning Tom arrives on Capitol Hill and walks into the cramped office suite he will share with the eleven staff members he inherited from Roger Blake. Tom introduces himself to his aides.

He then heads to his office to meet with his chief of staff, Cassie Rivera, a tall dark-skinned brunette in her late forties, with her hair cut short and straight. Blake had described Cassie as "a Wharton MBA who discovered that politics is more interesting than business. She's tough and pragmatic, the perfect person to run the office. Just don't call her Connie or Constance, her real name. She hates it." Blake had also said that Cassie's parents were Cuban and she was married to an architect who was part Korean and part African-American. They did not have any children.

"Roger praised you to the skies," Tom tells her. "He said I'd learn more from you than from anyone else in this building. And I'd like you to give me a full briefing. But first I want to meet with each staff member for a few minutes. You know, reassure them. I don't want them to feel rattled about being handed a new boss out of the blue."

"Don't reassure them too much," says Cassie. "A little fear will motivate them to work harder."

Tom laughs and asks Cassie to send in Jeffrey Lazlo, Blake's legislative aide. Blake had portrayed Jeffrey as "a very bright and tireless researcher. His Harvard masters in public administration was often an asset. But sometimes his idealism got in the way." Jeffrey walks briskly into Tom's office, his glasses slightly askew. He has the lean build of a runner. Tom asks how he came to Washington.

"My passion for politics began in grade school," Jeffrey replies. "I was fascinated by my parents' stories of life in communist Hungary. They fled during the 1956 uprising against Soviet rule."

"By comparison," says Tom, "our country's problems must not seem so serious."

"They're serious enough," says Jeffrey.

"I agree," says Tom. "Public education, for instance. It's a disgrace. Making it work is my top priority. I also worry that Social Security and Medicare will ruin this country's finances. We've got to do something about them."

"Yes," says Jeffrey, his eyes widening. "Congressman Blake was pretty cautious about those issues. He let me pitch lots of ideas and let me write plenty of position papers, but he stuffed most of them into his desk drawer. I doubt if he read past the first page. To tell you the truth, I nearly quit several times. But if you want to make a real difference here, I want to help."

Tom lays out his priorities on other major issues and asks Jeffrey to draft new position papers. Jeffrey leaves with more spring in his step than he had when he came in.

Tom meets briefly with his other staff members and then calls Cassie back into his office. "What do you suggest I focus on first?" he asks.

"The next election. It's only nine months away," Cassie replies. "We don't have the usual two years to do all the things that could boost your odds of winning a second time. Plus, in November, five times as many voters will show up as did for the special election last week, and many more kinds of voters will go to the polls. The campaign will be a lot tougher. You need to know what your constituents care about."

"I've lived there for fourteen years," Tom replies. "I have a good sense of the place."

"An overall feel is fine," says Cassie, "but the details often matter more. For instance, I assume you know that our district has about 30,000 households in each income bracket from $10,000 to $50,000. Plus 80,000 households fill higher brackets."

"I got the sense that voters in the district were all over the lot economically," says Tom. "For instance, when I questioned whether we should keep the

Bush tax cuts, I got roughly equal amounts of heat and praise. Upper-middle-class voters mostly protested, while voters earning less cheered me on. On most issues, the district struck me as ending up in the middle of the road."

"Sort of," says Cassie, smiling. "About 100,000 people fall into each camp: conservative, moderate, and liberal. The rest, nobody can really peg. We're a real grab bag."

"During my campaign, I noticed that hardly anyone asked where I stood on Medicare or Social Security," says Tom. "How do you see our district shaping up on those subjects?"

Cassie shrugs. "Any stand you take can get you in trouble. If seniors think you want to cut their benefits, you're toast. And if you propose to cut benefits or raise taxes in the future, younger generations will come after your scalp. You're better off saying nothing."

"But we can't sit back and do nothing," says Tom. "Social Security and Medicare are going to implode."

"Someday, the voters who ought to be worrying about that will make themselves heard at the polls," says Cassie. "Until then, you need to stay away from those subjects."

"That's not my style," says Tom.

"With all due respect, Congressman, if you want to stay on Capitol Hill, you will have to choose your issues carefully. On plenty of subjects, you simply can't win."

"I understand," says Tom. "Even on the issue I know best, I had to tread lightly. I proposed spending more money to upgrade public education, thinking everyone would expect that from me. Yet folks without kids in public schools fumed at the idea, while the parents of school kids criticized me for not wanting to spend even more."

"So you get my drift," says Cassie.

Tom nods. But he still believes that he can do what's right for the whole district—the young and the old, the well off and the poor, blue-collar and white-collar workers. After he takes positions on important bills, though, what will his voters think? Will they still believe that he's standing up for them? Tom wonders how other folks in Congress deal with that. But he is uncomfortable asking any of the old pros how they deal with their constituents, until he better understands the challenges himself.

So Tom decides to do some research on his own by calling the Library of Congress. The clerk recommends a book by a professor who traveled with eighteen lawmakers to observe their interactions with voters. The book is titled *Home Style: House Members in Their Districts*. Tom has it sent to his office and skims through it. He then calls the author, Richard Fenno, who sounds more down-to-earth than most academics Tom has encountered.

In response to Tom's questions, Fenno says that most legislators avoid discussing issues in depth with their voters. Instead, the typical incumbent focuses on presenting himself as trustworthy, hardworking, and accessible. A typical lawmaker implies to voters, "I am one of you, so you can trust me to make the right decisions."

Tom then asks, "How do incumbents deal with issues superficially yet win reelection more than 90 percent of the time?"

Fenno replies that most members of Congress cultivate an inner circle of supporters who provide time, money, and advice, all of which give incumbents a big edge over challengers.

Troubled by Fenno's description of how most lawmakers deal with their constituents, Tom heads back to the library and checks out other books on the subject.

One of them disturbs him even more. It claims that incumbents keep their jobs indefinitely mainly because of name recognition.

When Tom asks Cassie about that, she answers, "That's more or less true. Let me show you a website." She points to Tom's computer. When he nods, Cassie logs on to the American National Election Studies site. "Notice that 42 percent of voters can recall the local incumbent's name, but only 17 percent can recall the challenger's. People naturally vote for the name they know. So any incumbent has a huge edge."

"How exactly do incumbents stay in the public eye?" Tom asks.

"Most spend big blocks of time back in their districts meeting with constituents. For most members of Congress, that's the number one priority," Cassie replies. "And even when they're in Washington, most lawmakers spend more time meeting with voters than on any other activity."

Tom wonders what they do in those sessions. But rather than hearing secondhand from Cassie, Tom feels ready to ask a colleague directly. He calls Fran Sinclair, the House member whom Blake had said to look up and whose office is just down the hall. Her chief of staff tells Tom that she's just left. "You might catch her on the way out. She's wearing a bright red coat. You can't miss her."

Tom walks into the hall, spots the coat, and sprints to catch Fran. She's as tall as Tom is and very thin. She holds her head high like someone used to the limelight. When Tom introduces himself, her stride doesn't slow down one bit. She shakes his hand, welcoming him to the club. Tom mentions that Blake spoke highly of her. "Good man," she exclaims. "Roger knew how to keep his constituents happy."

"Glad you mentioned that," Tom says. "He said you could tell me more about that subject than almost anyone here."

"That's probably so. But I gotta go now," Fran says, speeding up. "I can meet you at 5:30. Let's make it at Johnny's Half Shell. Do you know where it is?"

"I'll find it."

That evening Tom arrives on the dot. Waiting for Fran, he orders a cup of coffee. She comes in twenty minutes late, speaking into a cell phone. "You'll be fine, I promise. See you Saturday. Bye."

She sits down and tells Tom, "My grandson had a nasty fall and needed stitches. He's tough, though, like me."

A waiter approaches, and Fran orders a Dewar's.

"Okay," she says, fixing her eyes on Tom's. "Tell me: do you want to be here for the short term or the long haul?"

"I didn't turn my life upside down just to be here for nine months."

"Good. If you want to keep your job, you've got to visit your district every weekend, not the twice a month that's typical. You have only nine months to make an impression. People have to see your face and hear your name. You need to talk at Rotary Clubs and any other local group that'll have you. Speak at high school graduations and church groups. Get your smiling face in the papers. Get your voice heard on local radio. Press the flesh. See and be seen."

Her scotch arrives. She sips it intently. "On a weekend when your district has no meetings scheduled that it makes sense for you to attend, hold a town meeting of your own and invite everyone in the area. Even people who don't go will get the invitations, see your name, and get the feeling that you care. If a weekend comes and you can't go home, we have a high-tech studio and satellite link on the Hill, so TV stations in your district can interview you."

She takes another sip of scotch and continues, "And use the mails. At government expense, you can send folks back home a constant stream of newsletters that keep them aware of your name and what you're doing for them."

"Unlimited mail at no cost. Isn't that a privilege that's easy to abuse?"

"Your job—part of it, anyway—is to keep your constituents informed," Fran replies. "Your voters want to know that someone is looking out for them."

"But if all the information is about my activities, isn't that just self-promotion?"

"This ain't the Boy Scouts, my friend. Look, if your conscience bothers you, there are plenty of ways to truly help people yet still boost your odds of getting reelected. You can assist voters in dealing with the federal bureaucracy, give them a hand on problems with Social Security, get your staff to give them tours of Capitol Hill, help their kids get into West Point, assist them with applications for government jobs or grants, and so on. Those you help will feel obligated to you. And even if they backed your opponent in the last election, they'll be more likely to vote for you the next time around. Plus they'll tell their friends and neighbors how much your office did for them."

"I saw that half my staff was assigned to constituent services."

"Right. And check out Blake's website. The most prominent button on his home page encourages voters to contact his office for help." Fran then flips on her cell phone. "That's it for now. I gotta run. If you want more tips, I have a few minutes to spare before lunch tomorrow. Just stop by my office."

The next morning, Tom checks out several of his colleagues' websites. They all highlight constituent services. Tom hears a knock at the door. It's Jeffrey.

Looking at Tom's computer screen, Jeffrey says, "You can drown in that stuff. Lots of people around here complain that constituent services constantly distract them from working on the issues that really matter. Speaking of which, can I bend your ear about some ideas I have for those position papers you wanted?"

"Can you hold off until this afternoon?" Tom asks. "Then I can devote my full attention to it. There are a few things I want to clear up first."

Later, Tom stops by Fran's office. Her walls are covered with photographs of her standing next to people of various kinds, from a high school basketball team to the president.

"I have one more tip for you," Fran begins. "Make sure your district gets its share of federal money. Whenever you obtain projects that your voters can see, it's a great way to remind them of your name."

Tom sits up straight in his chair. "I promised my voters I wouldn't waste their tax dollars. I meant it. I won't squander their money on projects whose main purpose is to keep me in office."

Fran scowls. "For every item that the press calls 'pork,' I can point to some voters who really care about it. Every federal project does some good."

"Many do a tiny amount of good at a huge price," says Tom. "What about that bridge in Alaska that would have linked an island of 50 people to a town of 8,000 at a cost of $250 million? That worked out to more than $30,000 for each person who could use the bridge. It would have been cheaper to give each one $10,000 in cash. And they'd all surely have preferred the cash. What a waste."

"The chair of the House Transportation Committee got funding for that item. I admit it was over the top."

"But I've heard about many other items that blatantly wasted tax dollars. What was the pressing national purpose for the museum in North Carolina devoted to teapots, the memorial in Massachusetts to Dr. Seuss, and all those buildings in Pennsylvania named for Bud Shuster?"

"Bud was also the chair of the House Transportation Committee. That position offers too much temptation for anyone to ignore."

"Are you saying that it's just a few committee chairs who fritter away tax-payers' money? How, then, do you explain that *Newsweek* once calculated that Congress spends $100 billion a year on projects that benefit the 535 members here more than the 300 million other citizens?"

"Listen to me," says Fran. "If you crusade against other members' projects, if you try to kill items that you think are excessive, the lawmakers who sponsored those projects will have it in for you and the bills you sponsor. You'll get nothing done here."

Tom shifts in his chair.

"I have one last thought for you," Fran says. "Whatever stand you take on Social Security, taxes, education, or any other issue that you're burning to do some good on will get you in trouble with some bloc of voters back home. But if you bring a project to your district, voters won't object to that. So I recommend that you get off your high horse."

Tom thanks her for the candid advice and walks back toward his office, deep in thought. When he spots Jeffrey and Cassie outside his door, he recounts his conversation with Fran.

"She forgot to tell you something," Cassie says. "Most people here for the first time vow to run lily white election campaigns. But to get reelected, you'll probably have to slam your opponent."

"I hate that stuff," Tom declares. "I hate negative campaigning."

"It stinks. But at times, you have to use it," Cassie says. "You can't win on the issues alone. You can't simultaneously please middle-class voters and the poor, the young and the old, families and singles, high school dropouts and PhDs. Any stand you take on a hot issue will tick off huge blocs of voters—if you insist on telling them where you really stand. It'll be much easier and more effective for us to paint an image of your opponent as a creep."

Jeffrey pipes in, "Wait a minute, Cassie. There are ways we can give every bloc of voters a fair shake." Then, to Tom, "For instance, this morning I wanted to talk with you about our position on Social Security. A group called the National Commission on Retirement Policy has published the most practical solution I've seen. It's not painless, but it is fair to everyone."

"Get serious," says Cassie. "Who's going to take the trouble to understand a complex set of recommendations? How long is this commission's report?"

"Fifty pages or so."

"It must be a real fun read," says Cassie. "And you could never condense the proposals into a thirty-second sound bite that voters would find appealing."

"I could give it a shot."

"Don't waste your time," says Cassie. "Plenty of smart people have tried to make Social Security reform sound attractive. Either they gave up or they lied about what their reforms would cost. But I can find a few accurate words about any election opponent that will make him look like a total rat. Plus that image will stick in people's minds far longer than your intricate ideas about public policy."

"I won't resort to mudslinging," says Tom. "I campaigned on the issues."

"You said you didn't discuss Social Security and Medicare," Cassie responds. "I'll bet you didn't deal with many other hot button issues."

"Well . . ."

"What's more," Cassie interrupts, "in a special election like yours, turnout is very low. Mostly the party faithful show up. Next time, there'll be many more voters and many more types of voters. It'll be a real brawl."

Tom protests. "It doesn't have to be that way. Remember the debates before the first few presidential primaries in 2008? The candidates talked mostly about their policy differences. And they did it civilly."

"Early on, sure," says Cassie, "because in each party, *several* candidates had a shot to win. Among the Democrats, for instance, Hillary Clinton, Barack Obama, and John Edwards were in serious contention. So if Clinton had started out attacking Obama too harshly, voters would have been turned off to Clinton and Obama, which would have mostly helped Edwards. Clinton wasn't about to do that. But once she and Obama were the only contenders left, the whole situation changed. The race turned nasty."

"She's right," says Jeffrey. "A two-person race tends to be ugly. After all, if the contest is only between you and one other challenger, all you have to do to win is make the other candidate look worse. And mud does that job very well. It usually hurts the person it lands on more than the one who threw it."

"I didn't come to Washington to hurl insults," Tom declares. "I came here to get something done."

"No one here likes mudslinging," says Cassie. "Voters detest it. But it works. The proof is it's becoming more common. I've seen statistics that negative ads were about 20 percent of the total in the 1970s. Now, most political ads are negative. I have a cartoon on my desk that shows an out-of-work campaign manager carrying a sign 'Will Be Negative for Food.'"

Tom smiles, briefly. "Cassie, you may be right. But for now, I want to focus on the issues that matter."

Cassie rolls her eyes. "All your opponent will need to do is tie your name to something really ugly. If he does it right, your own mother won't vote for you. You'll be out of a job. So will we."

"I'll deal with that when it's time to campaign in September. For now, I'll take *some* of Fran's advice and spend the weekend in the district. Let's find places for me to speak. I'd like to start at my old high school. I'm sure the new principal will let me use one of the rooms for an evening."

Cassie nods, grudgingly.

That Friday, Tom heads home. The tree-lined streets, single-family houses, and kids playing in the snow feel more inviting to him than Washington's imposing architecture.

Arriving at his former high school, Tom feels more relaxed than he has at any time since he left. Kelley is waiting in the entranceway, smiling. After a hug, they head for the conference room on the first floor. About sixty people are present, from young couples to seniors. Tom recognizes many of them. After circulating for a few minutes, he heads to the front of the room and thanks everyone for being there and for giving him the chance to represent them.

Tom then says, "Many folks I've met in Washington warned me that I'd get in trouble if I spoke the truth about the tough issues. I don't buy that. I believe that you expect me to tell you the truth as I see it, and I will. For instance, I think the biggest threat to American prosperity isn't foreign competition. Instead, it's two programs that are on course to consume the entire federal budget and bankrupt this country. I'm talking about Social Security and Medicare. We have to fix both programs, and we can. We can keep them financially sound while still being fair to both retirees and workers. After all, people keep living longer than ever. So, we can steadily raise the retirement age without harming anyone. And many folks have other sources of income, so we can safely limit their Social Security and Medicare benefits." Though he has more to say, Tom notices that the once friendly faces are starting to turn cold, so he asks if there are any questions.

A woman of about fifty says, "In effect, you want to deprive me of the benefits that every senior now takes for granted."

"I'm just trying to deal with the issue honestly and fairly . . . "

"What do you mean by fair?" a white-haired man shouts. "Yuppies today live twice as well as I ever did. Don't tell me that when I retire they can't afford to pay the small amount I'll need to live on plus my basic health care. They can afford it much more than I can afford to lose any benefits that I've paid Social Security taxes all my life to get. My small pension—what you call other sources of income—won't be enough."

The youngest person in the crowd, a man of about thirty, blurts out, "What you're really saying is that people my age should cough up record amounts of Social Security taxes, with no shot to get back what retirees today think is owed to them. Under your plan, I wouldn't get a check until I'm too old to spend it."

Tom's face burns from the criticism being hurled at him. He thanks the crowd for speaking the truth as they see it and promises to give their input more thought.

On the drive home, Kelley tries to console him. Tom responds, "Let's talk about something else. This is just a break-in period I have to go through."

That night, he gets blistering calls from campaign supporters.

At his public meeting the next day, Tom talks in platitudes. When he takes questions, most people ask for help with personal matters concerning some federal agency. Tom promises each one that one of his aides will get back to them.

On the plane back to Washington Sunday night, Tom realizes that he didn't even touch on other issues that concern him. He and Jeffrey had put together several creative ideas for improving public education. Yet Tom fears that conservative voters in his district would blast every proposal as intruding into an area that rightfully belongs to the states, while liberal voters would scorn the ideas as inadequate for an issue so important that it required a major federal investment. Tom shakes his head in frustration.

On his way into the office the following day, Tom hears a familiar footstep behind him in the hallway. It's Fran.

"I hear you had a rough time this weekend," she says. "Sounds like some of your constituents would have lobbed pipe bombs if they'd had the chance."

"How did you hear about that?"

"Oh, word gets around here fast. Besides, I have a vested interest. The party's campaign committee wants me to keep an eye on you. I'm supposed to be giving you good advice."

"I just told the truth. I tried to be fair to all sides. Isn't that what my constituents want?"

"They say they do, but the people who go to these meetings have axes to grind," Fran says. "And each group has its own demands that clash with other groups' needs. You can't possibly please them. If you take stands on the hard issues, you'll just make people mad. So don't dwell on the hard issues."

"What if people ask me where I stand?"

"Talk in generalities," Fran replies. "Reduce your stand to a slogan. Jimmy Carter, in his winning presidential campaign, said his foreign policy would be as great as the American people. But he didn't reveal what his foreign policy would actually be."

"Don't my constituents expect real answers?"

"Then give them one. The answer is, 'It's the other party's fault.' Tell them the other party blocks real solutions. Say the other party panders to special interests. Haven't you noticed that Republicans and Democrats constantly throw rocks at each other over Social Security, Medicare, taxes, the environment, and every other divisive issue? Why do you think that is?"

"You're going to tell me, I'm sure."

"Blaming the other side is just easier and safer than trying to deal with the tough issues," Fran says. "Didn't this weekend's meetings teach you that political fact of life?"

"I'm learning it the hard way," says Tom. "I appreciate your candor."

Tom trudges back to his office. He tells his secretary that he doesn't want to be disturbed and closes the door behind him. On his desk, he sees Jeffrey's preliminary position papers. Flipping through them, Tom likes many of Jeffrey's ideas. But for each proposal, Tom envisions some bloc of voters who would blast him for taking that stand. Tom puts the papers aside and picks up a memo from Cassie on how to make constituent services more efficient. As Tom turns the first page, he realizes that he's avoiding the hard policy stuff.

Tom leans back in his chair, scowling. In office less than a week, yet he's shrinking from the issues that most trouble him—out of fear that if he faces them head-on, some bloc of voters will lash out at him. Tom shudders at the thought that he has already started to become the kind of politician he hates.

He won't allow himself to go down that road. He can't take the path that Cassie and Fran have laid out for him. He puts down Cassie's memo.

To clear his head, Tom leaves his office for a walk in the cold winter air. He sits down on a bench, looking at the traces of snow left over from the last storm. He wonders, How did it end up this way—that lawmakers are constantly squeezed between doing what they think is right and what will get them reelected?

Tom decides to ask Jeffrey to research that question and write up a memo. He'll tell Jeffrey to pull no punches. No sugar coating. With some hard facts in front of him and some hard-nosed thinking, maybe he can figure a way out of this bind.

5

How Did American Politics
Get So Dysfunctional?

Eight days later, Tom walks into his office at 7:30 a.m., arriving before anyone else. He's trying to stay on top of his job, even while he wonders whether he can do it in a way that he believes in. Taking off his coat, Tom sees yet another memo on his desk. This one, though, is what he's been waiting for. Tom loosens his tie and sits down to read—focused, intent.

TO: Rep. Tom Hennessey
FROM: Jeffrey Lazlo
SUBJECT: Every Legislator's Bind

Two centuries ago, America's founders anticipated the dilemma you're in now. They knew that every lawmaker would be torn between catering to his constituents' expectations and serving the country's best interests.

The framers also saw how to resolve the quandary—so that legislators could do both jobs properly. Each representative would just need to speak for a group of citizens who shared common political interests. Each lawmaker could then lucidly explain to his voters how his actions in Congress served those interests, if in fact his actions did.

That is how this institution worked—at first. In the early 1800s, a typical House member represented mostly farmers. Each legislator knew his constituents' needs in detail.

But after the Civil War, many Americans began to work in offices and factories, a trend that accelerated over time. Each lawmaker thus began representing more kinds of people.

By now, in our day, the residents of any district work at a wider variety of jobs than anyone 200 years ago could have imagined, from steel workers to computer programmers. Our lifestyles also vary far more than ever, from apartment buildings filled with singles, couples, families, you-name-it, to nursing homes filled with seniors. Each district now includes so many kinds of people with such different expectations and needs that no one representative could possibly satisfy them.

The founders would undoubtedly object. They believed that each lawmaker should speak for a bloc of citizens whose interests and values he clearly grasps. So the founders would surely argue that representing a district no longer makes sense. They would disapprove of how the House is currently organized.

Most Americans would no doubt be surprised. But the framers' plans are clear for anyone to see in *The Federalist Papers* and James Madison's notes on the Constitutional Convention. Here, briefly, is what those records reveal about the founders' intentions:

Tom stops reading. He, too, is surprised by this description of what the founders intended for Congress. To focus better, Tom gets a cup of coffee from the kitchenette. He then sits down to read the rest of the memo to see how Jeffrey backs up his claims.

When the framers began to draft the Constitution, they split into several camps. One side argued that citizens should have all political power, with the government acting as the public's servant. James Wilson even insisted that the only reason to have a Congress was that the American people couldn't possibly meet in one place to make policy decisions themselves. So, Wilson added, each lawmaker "ought to speak the language of his constituents" and vote on issues exactly as they would.

Other founders had less faith in the common man. They feared that most citizens would focus on their own needs and wants, not on what was best for the nation overall. So those framers, including Roger Sherman and Elbridge Gerry, advocated that the members of Congress report to their state legislatures, not to ordinary citizens.

As James Madison saw it, though, politicians weren't angels, no more than voters were. All were flesh and blood. All could make mistakes. But politicians had far more power than most, power they could abuse. So to ensure that lawmakers served America's best interests, Madison argued, citizens had to have power over them.

He won that debate. Madison persuaded his fellow delegates at the Constitutional Convention that ordinary citizens should elect members of the House. Voters could then evaluate their representative on a regular basis. If they didn't trust him or they didn't support his decisions, they could boot him out of office.

How, though, would each lawmaker keep his voters' trust? How would he connect with them strongly enough to keep his job? Each representative would have to know "the interests and circumstances of his constituents." He would have to look out for their welfare.

Each representative could easily carry out that task—in Madison's time—because the voters within any district had remarkably similar interests. Eighty percent of early Americans worked on farms; 80 percent also lived in families with five or more members; and 90 percent were under the age of forty-five.

What's more, the voters in each region often had a similar slant on issues of the day. Northerners mostly opposed slavery, while southern whites insisted on retaining it. Meanwhile, farmers in the North and South wanted to export their crops and import manufactured goods. So they sought to keep import duties low. People in more commercial areas, though, wanted to protect their livelihoods from foreign competitors. They sought higher tariffs. In each district, then, the representative knew what his constituents expected.

Even so, Madison predicted that Congress would act in the nation's overall interests. It would "refine and enlarge the public views." It would focus on the big picture. Madison justified his optimism by asserting that Congress would contain so many competing interests that no small clique of lawmakers with self-serving agendas could dominate the proceedings.

Madison's expectations were surely also based on his own experiences as a legislator. He knew that any member of the House who wanted to do his constituents any good would have to resolve differences with other lawmakers. To advance his own agenda, a representative would have to help others advance theirs. To pass a controversial bill, lawmakers from across the country would have to see benefits from it.

Each representative could then return home to show the residents of his district how the measures he had worked on would benefit them. Since most of his constituents shared a similar outlook on the major issues, he could frame a coherent message. He could make a solid case for his decisions.

In time, though, that scenario had to break down. Madison foresaw that it would. He knew that many of us would eventually work at desks and machines in various kinds of industries. At that point, our interests would be far more diverse than when 80 percent of us were farmers. And as the country industrialized, the issues that politicians had to address would become more complex.

Madison was right, of course. The issues changed dramatically and so have the American people. After the Civil War, corporations grew in size and power. As a result, the poor collided more often with the middle class, and both collided more often with the rich. Progressives opposed laissez-faire capitalists. Communities ended up more divided than ever over the major issues. (I have more information about that trend, if you're interested.)*

By now, when it comes to the top issues, where a citizen lives hardly counts. Just think of the topics that most Americans worry about today:

The economy

National security

Health care

Social Security

Taxes

For these subjects, where one lives is largely irrelevant. What matters are a person's political values, income, age, and family situation.

And people vary by income, age, and family situation far more than in the country's early years. We've shifted from a fairly homogeneous society at the start to a very diverse country today. (I have more data about that trend too, if you want to see it.)†

* Appendix II.

† Appendix III.

Americans have become so diverse that a lawmaker's job is nothing like what the founders intended. Your constituents span every type of household, income bracket, age group, and ideological camp. It's as if you had to represent all of America at once. How could anyone do that job?

The good news is that the founders let us design the House to fit our needs at each point in time. The Constitution doesn't require the House to represent districts. The Constitution doesn't even *mention* districts. It lets each state decide how to elect its own House members, although Congress can revise what the states do.

But we have not taken advantage of that flexibility. From the start, nearly every member of the House has represented all the residents of a district. Then in 1967, Congress required that every state use that arrangement (perhaps because incumbents win that kind of election more than 90 percent of the time).

The founders would surely disapprove. They envisioned that each House member would speak for a bloc of voters who shared common interests.

That idea would no doubt strike many people today as radical. Your fellow lawmakers would consider it downright subversive. So, perhaps, we should sit down to talk about these findings. I'll bring along *The Federalist Papers* and Madison's notes on the Constitutional Convention.* You'll see what the framers intended. Each House member was supposed to represent a politically coherent bloc of citizens.

Tom shakes his head, thinking he'd have been better off working on Capitol Hill 200 years ago. His voters would have been in much closer sync with him. Yet he also feels hopeful. Having learned that the founders wanted each lawmaker to have a genuine bond with his constituents, Tom wonders if he can use that bit of history to help create that kind of bond today. To explore the possibilities and figure out what to do next, Tom decides to sit down with Jeffrey early that morning.

---

* Excerpts in Appendix IV.

6

Each District as Diverse as the Whole United States

Jeffrey braces himself for the storm to come. He knows that Cassie will lash out at him. She and Roger Blake had lambasted him whenever he pushed big ideas and whenever he ventured beyond the political reality of the moment. They had demoralized Jeffrey enough that he had often considered leaving Capitol Hill. He had stayed because his girlfriend Rachel and his parents kept encouraging his desire to make a difference. Tom Hennessey seemed to be in that camp too. Unfortunately, it was the Roger Blakes and Fran Sinclairs who dominated Congress, which made Jeffrey worry that both he and Tom would eventually give up.

As Jeffrey walks into Tom's office mulling over what lies ahead, he spots Cassie, who does just what he expects. She instantly goes on the attack.

"Your memo about the founders' intentions might please your former professors. But here, it's useless."

Before Jeffrey can respond, Tom interjects, "The memo sounded reasonable to me. Why do you think it's of no value?"

"None of it is doable," Cassie replies. "Imagine if we told our constituents what Jeffrey has in mind. Imagine if we publicly advocated that our country end its 200-year-old practice of one representative speaking for each district. People would look at us as if we were crazy. Nearly everyone believes that 'All politics is local.'"

"National politics isn't 'local' anymore," says Tom. "Our district is so divided over Social Security, Medicare, and a whole bunch of other issues that you warned me not to discuss them. You also threw statistics at me about how we're evenly split between conservatives, liberals, and moderates. Plus our people are all over the lot economically."

Cassie shoots back: "We can't turn Congress upside down simply because our district is tough to figure out. The fact is most districts have a distinct character. Southern Florida is jammed with seniors. Los Angeles overflows with young people. Suburbia is mostly families. Cities have lots of singles and single parents. Some neighborhoods are posh. Others are impoverished. In a typical district, the residents have plenty in common."

"That's what most people think," Jeffrey says. "But it's flat out wrong. Nearly every district is as diverse as the whole country. I have the Census data to prove it." He pulls papers out of a folder. "As you'll see, each district contains hordes of folks in every age group, every household category, every job type, even every income level."

"That can't be right," says Cassie. "The state legislatures have drawn nearly every congressional district so that it's either solidly Republican or solidly Democratic. Districts can't have the same characteristics."

"I didn't say they were the same," says Jeffrey. "Each place varies from the average in some respect. But each district is still roughly as diverse as the whole country. After all, each district has to have more than 600,000 people, which means it has to include several neighborhoods. And neighborhoods vary—a lot. So each district ends up with hordes of folks in every demographic group."

"I still don't believe it," says Cassie.

"Then look at the Census data I've put together," says Jeffrey, waving a chart at her. "Take the largest age group, people in their mid-twenties to mid-forties. They make up 30 percent of the U.S. And, in 85 percent of districts, they're between 27 to 33 percent of the total."

"Huh," Cassie responds.

"The same applies in *every* age bracket," says Jeffrey. "Just check out the numbers. In most districts, each age group is about the same proportion of the population as in the whole U.S."

Percent of People in Each Age Bracket		
AGE BRACKET	PERCENT OF U.S. POPULATION	PERCENT OF POPULATION IN 85% OF CONGRESSIONAL DISTRICTS
0–14	21%	18–25%
15–24	14%	11–17%
25–44	30%	27–33%
45–64	22%	19–24%
65 and over	12%	8–16%

Cassie looks at the chart, snorts, and hands it to Tom.

"No wonder Congress can't do anything sane about Medicare or Social Security," Tom says. "Every one of my colleagues has to deal with large numbers of constituents in every age group, each with its own ax to grind."

"Afraid so," says Jeffrey.

"On most issues, though, other factors matter more than age," says Cassie. "For instance, whether people have kids. The proportion that do must vary from place to place."

"Not as much as you seem to think," Jeffrey replies smiling, pulling out a second chart. "Married couples with kids make up a quarter of the U.S. And, in 85 percent of districts, families with kids are at least two-thirds of that figure. The same holds true in the other household categories. Just look."

Percent of Households in Each Family Category		
HOUSEHOLD TYPE	PERCENT OF U.S. POPULATION	PERCENT OF POPULATION IN 85% OF CONGRESSIONAL DISTRICTS
Married with children	24%	16–32%
Married without children	28%	21–34%
Nontraditional family (mostly single parents)	16%	10–22%
Nonfamily (mostly singles)	32%	24–39%

"Okay," says Cassie, peering at the second chart. "But occupations vary from region to region. We've got the Farm Belt, the Rust Belt, Silicon Valley, and so on."

"Industries vary from place to place," Jeffrey says. "But the broad job categories don't. What I mean is that the number of professionals, managers, administrators, laborers, and craftsmen is roughly the same from district to district. See . . . "

Percent of Workers in Each Job Category		
JOB CATEGORY	**PERCENT OF U.S. POPULATION**	**PERCENT OF POPULATION IN 85% OF CONGRESSIONAL DISTRICTS**
Professional/Manager	34%	25–43%
Administrative Support	27%	24–30%
Craftsmen	9%	8–12%
Service & Labor	30%	21–38%
Farmers	1%	0–2%

"I'd bet that everyone on the Hill would be surprised by these numbers," says Tom.

"Probably," says Cassie. "But notice that Jeffrey's charts leave out 15 percent of the districts. I'll bet those vary from the norm."

"Again, not as much as you seem to think," says Jeffrey. "I have other charts for 98 percent of districts. And in nearly every age, job, and household category, the proportion of people is at least half of what it is for the United States as a whole. Want to see those numbers?"*

"Maybe later," says Tom. "You've made your point. We can see that the typical district contains people of all kinds."

"When it comes to incomes, though, Jeffrey's thesis falls apart," says Cassie. "Some places are poor. Some are rich. Some are middle class."

"That's a myth," says Jeffrey. "Only a handful of districts are predominantly poor and almost none are predominantly rich. Most districts have their population spread almost *evenly* across the whole range of incomes."

"Really?" asks Tom. "Show us."

Jeffrey pulls out another chart:

---

* Appendix V.

Percent of Households in Each Income Bracket		
INCOME BRACKET	PERCENT OF U.S. POPULATION	PERCENT OF POPULATION IN 85% OF CONGRESSIONAL DISTRICTS
Less than $10K	10%	5–16%
$10K–20K	13%	8–18%
$20K–30K	13%	10–17%
$30K–40K	12%	10–14%
$40K–50K	11%	9–12%
$50K–60K	9%	8–11%
$60K–75K	10%	8–13%
$75K–99K	10%	6–14%
More than $100K	12%	4–21%

"Notice that most districts have about 10 percent of their households in *each* income bracket," says Jeffrey. "*Only* at the very top and bottom brackets does the proportion of people deviate much from 10 percent. The typical district couldn't be more economically diverse."

"What about the 15 percent of districts that this chart leaves out?" asks Cassie.

"Again, it's only in the very low or high brackets that the proportion of people deviates much from 10 percent. Look."

Percent of Households in Each Income Bracket		
INCOME BRACKET	PERCENT OF U.S. POPULATION	PERCENT OF POPULATION IN 98% OF CONGRESSIONAL DISTRICTS
Less than $10K	10%	2–19%
$10K–20K	13%	5–20%
$20K–30K	13%	7–18%
$30K–40K	12%	8–15%
$40K–50K	11%	8–13%
$50K–60K	9%	7–11%
$60K–75K	10%	7–14%
$75K–99K	10%	5–17%
More than $100K	12%	3–32%

"I know that some districts are poor and some are rich," says Cassie. "You gotta give me that."

Jeffrey laughs. "I grant that some places are richer than most, and some are poorer than most. But even in the richest districts, most people *aren't* rich. And in the poorest districts, nearly half the people *aren't* poor."

"How do you figure that?"

"Just look at the chart," says Jeffrey. "The households earning less than $30,000, the figures in boldface, are at most 57 percent of any district. So even in the poorest areas, 43 percent of the people are middle class or prosperous."

"I get it," says Cassie.

"Meanwhile, the households earning more than $75,000, the figures in italics, are at most 49 percent of any district. So even in the richest areas, most residents are middle class or poor."

"Aha," says Cassie. "That means the typical district is mostly middle class. So a typical representative can say that he speaks for the middle class."

"Okay," says Jeffrey. "But being middle class doesn't predict anyone's politics. A person's age, job, and type of household matter just as much. And there are more than a hundred ways to combine income level, age, job, and household type. For instance, every district has young, middle-class, professional single parents; poor, elderly, blue-collar couples. . . . Should I go on?"

"Please don't," says Cassie.

"But you do see Jeffrey's point?" Tom asks. "It's that each of those hundred-plus groups has its own mix of political interests."

"Yeah."

"Yet," says Jeffrey, "each member of Congress has to represent all those groups—just about every combination of wealth, age, family, and job type. How can anyone represent that wide an array of people?"

"I certainly bombed last week when I claimed to voters back home that I was looking out for all of them," says Tom.

Cassie shakes her head. "I still say that most districts have a distinct character. A city jammed with people and tall buildings is another world compared to a rural area filled with trees and streams."

"Sure," says Jeffrey, "but the overall sense of a place doesn't describe its residents. A community may be urban or rural, prosperous or seedy, but that can't capture the huge variety of people who live there. Just consider your own neighborhood. Bethesda is suburban and upscale. Yet, when you overhear people discussing taxes, homeland security, or any other issue, how many different outlooks do you catch wind of?"

"It gets pretty heated."

"And that's just among people you meet," says Jeffrey. "What about the more than 600,000 others in your district whom you rarely see? Some are starting out in life. Some are retired. Some make lots of money. Others barely make ends meet. Many have children. Others will never have kids. It goes on and on."

"So no congressperson can honestly claim to represent most district residents," says Tom.

"Exactly," says Jeffrey. "Any of your colleagues who backs a concrete solution to a hot issue can offend many groups in his home base. Naturally, most of your colleagues won't grapple with the big problems. Instead, they blame those problems on the other party."

"Nice speech," Cassie responds. "Everything you say may even be true. Some lawmakers hate having to appease a diverse bunch of voters. But most incumbents *love* the current setup. After all, more than 90 percent of incumbents keep winning reelection. They'll never make a big change."

"Most of my colleagues may want to keep things the way they are," says Tom, "but what about voters?"

"Most voters won't push for serious change," says Cassie.

"How can you be so sure?" asks Tom.

"Because," Jeffrey interjects, "she doesn't think much of the average American. But voters detest the current situation—enough to do plenty if someone showed them a change that would actually work. Most voters hunger for something better than what we have now."

"How much do they hunger for it?" asks Tom. "I want to know just how open voters are to big changes. I'd like you to research that question."

"I'll get right on it," says Jeffrey. Heading out the door, he feels more fired up than he has in years.

7

Why Do Most Voters Feel So Powerless?

"The system we now use for electing congresspeople turns off voters so much that most of them don't know or care who wins," Jeffrey says to Tom as they sit in his office.

"That is so over the top," says Cassie, shaking her head.

"It does sound extreme," says Tom. "How can most voters not care who wins?"

"Well," says Jeffrey, "remember when the Republicans won control of the House in 1994?"

"Of course," Tom replies. "They turned the country's politics inside out."

"So what percent of Americans do you think realized that the Republicans had won?" Jeffrey asks.

"No idea," Tom answers.

"By 2001, six years after that election, a Pew Research Center poll showed that 68 percent of voting-age Americans still didn't know that the Republicans held a majority in the House."

Tom groans.

"That's just the way things are," says Cassie. "Most voters have been out of it for as long as I've been here—especially when it comes to congressional elections."

"In the 2006 congressional election," Tom says, "Americans cared plenty—about the war in Iraq, about corruption."

"Did they?" asks Jeffrey. "Even in 2006, 60 percent of Americans eligible to vote didn't bother to. And most who did go to the polls reelected the same old faces—94 percent of incumbents won. Plus most voters knew almost nothing about where the candidates stood on the issues."

"How do you figure that?" asks Tom.

"In previous elections, American National Election Studies polls have shown that only 11 percent of voters could name *any* issue on which they knew how their representative had voted."

"It's been that way for a long time," says Cassie. "It's no big deal."

"The big deal is *why* voters care so little," says Jeffrey.

"Everyone knows why," says Cassie.

"Bull," says Jeffrey. "Even the so-called experts have no clue why voters are oblivious. What the big-name pundits say on this subject is complete nonsense. You'll see. Just let me add one more piece to the puzzle."

"Just one piece? Somehow, I doubt that," Cassie says.

"I want to hear what he's getting at," says Tom. "Go ahead, Jeffrey."

"The most in-depth survey to date of why voters go to the polls was carried out by Northwestern's School of Journalism after the 2000 election," says Jeffrey. He turns to Cassie, "Guess how many Americans said they voted because they liked or disliked the candidates?"

Cassie shrugs.

"Eleven percent," Jeffrey responds. "Only 11 percent of voters took the trouble to go to the polls because they cared about the candidates."

"Wait a minute," says Tom. "Plenty of voters care strongly about some issue. How can they care about any issue and not care about the candidates?"

"Because most people don't believe that their one vote has any effect on the issues."

"Then why do they show up?"

"Nearly 80 percent of voters said they went to the polls because they felt obligated to, wanted to exercise their civic rights, or were there out of habit," Jeffrey replies.

Tom shakes his head, frowning.

"Bad as that statistic sounds," says Cassie, "it doesn't back up Jeffrey's claim that voters are turned off by 'the system.' Most Americans are simply too lazy to learn about congressional candidates."

"No way," says Jeffrey. "Americans work longer hours than people in any other industrialized country. You've seen those studies. Lazy we're not."

"Maybe 'lazy' isn't the right word," Cassie says. "'Self-absorbed' is more like it. The average American is too busy chasing the almighty dollar and too preoccupied with family, friends, and having a good time to burden himself with Capitol Hill politics."

"That explains zip," says Jeffrey. "After all, if a guy cares mostly about himself and his family, who can he turn to if he wants a better job market, higher quality school, cleaner air and water, you name it? Who has power to improve any of those things? The tooth fairy? It's politicians who control all of that stuff."

"Absolutely," says Tom. "I'd expect people who are concerned about the quality of their own lives to be politically vigilant, not politically inert. To protect their own interests, I'd expect them to think hard about whom to vote for and to vote every time."

"Even if that's true," says Cassie, "people pay so little attention to the congressional candidates because they find politics so unsavory."

"That doesn't explain much," says Jeffrey. "If voters went to the polls mainly feeling repulsed by the status quo, they'd boot the incumbents out on their ears. Instead, over the last decade, Americans have reelected 97 percent of House incumbents."

"Then blame the media," says Cassie. "Television, radio, and newspapers paint such an ugly picture of American politics that most people try to put the whole subject out of their minds. That's why most people don't vote, and those who do vote just pick the name they know."

"The media give the public what it craves," says Jeffrey. "The media dish out what people will watch and read. They try to reflect the public's mood—more than they try to create it."

"Maybe," Cassie responds. "So what?"

"So the standard answers don't explain much about voter apathy," Jeffrey replies.

"Even if that's true, it doesn't mean 'the system' is to blame."

"Okay," says Jeffrey. "Now let me show you how our system *crushes* the average American's interest in voting and the candidates."

"How do you propose to show that?"

"By looking at a system that fires voters up."

"What are you talking about?" asks Cassie.

"In Europe, 80 percent of citizens vote in legislative elections, double the number here."

"And you think that's because . . . ?"

"Every country in continental Europe uses some form of proportional representation."

"Most Americans couldn't care less what Europeans do," says Cassie.

"If the vast majority of Europeans vote, while the vast majority of Americans don't, there must be something we can learn from that," says Tom.

"But Americans are used to the current arrangement," says Cassie. "They wouldn't give it up."

"Your great grandfather wouldn't give up his horse," Jeffrey responds, "but I'll bet that he changed his mind once he saw how much faster and more comfortably he could travel in a car."

"So are you suggesting that we should adopt European methods?" asks Cassie.

"Absolutely not," Jeffrey says. "European politics isn't noticeably better than ours. Some people say it's worse. But no one can say that about voter participation. On that score, proportional methods make our system look sick. So I'm suggesting that you have an open mind and take a look at what Europe does. That will help us pinpoint the flaws in *our* elections. It will help us figure out why most American voters don't give a damn about who they vote for."

"I want to hear that explanation," says Tom.

"Okay. Then let's look at proportional representation—for a minute," says Jeffrey. "Take Holland, which has the simplest proportional system. At each national election, each Dutch citizen can vote for one party, with eleven parties to choose from. Whatever percent of voters chooses each party, that's the percent of seats it wins in Parliament. If 20 percent of voters choose Party A, it gets 20 percent of the seats."

"We know all that," says Cassie, looking at Tom, who nods.

"But look at how it affects voters," says Jeffrey. "Every Dutch voter is represented by his or her chosen party. Every Dutch voter is represented for what matters to him politically."

"You think that makes a big difference?" asks Cassie.

"A huge difference," Jeffrey replies. "By contrast, every American has to share his or her representative with everyone else in the district. Every parent has to share a representative with singles, every blue-collar worker with moguls, every liberal with staunch conservatives, every young adult with seniors, and so on. Everyone in a district—despite their vast differences and disagreements—has to share the very *same* member of Congress. So the average citizen cannot possibly get a representative who reflects his own beliefs. Why, then, are we surprised that most Americans don't vote? Why are we surprised that most voters don't know beans about the candidates?"

"I can almost see your point," says Cassie. "But everyone else blames voter apathy on laziness, the media, and so on. Why are you the only person I know who blames the system?"

Tom interjects: "Because the system has always been this way. So most people take it for granted. As they say, 'Whoever discovered water, it wasn't a fish.' People constantly immersed in something simply don't see it."

"But if people are that steeped in the current system," says Cassie, "we'll never convince them that the system is what ruins their civic spirit."

"We just need to present the idea in the right way," says Jeffrey. "Imagine, for instance, if each of us was allowed to listen to only one musician that the majority in our district got to choose. Who would your district pick?"

"Probably some rapper," Cassie replies.

"Knowing how you feel about that stuff, you'd never turn on your radio again."

"Maybe."

"Or what if you could go to only one kind of restaurant that the majority favored? Isn't Italian food big where you live? You've told me that it gives your husband heartburn. So if that's what most folks wanted, the two of you would be stuck in your kitchen."

"Could be."

"Yet everyone in a district has to share the same political spokesperson," says Jeffrey. "Of course most of us give up on politics."

Cassie looks out the window for a long moment, then turns back to Jeffrey. "Suppose you're right. Do you think you can convince most people? Will they buy that the average American is politically inert for reasons they've never thought of?"

"We can convince folks if we put it in terms that grab them in the gut," Tom says.

"Like what?" asks Cassie.

"We just need to tie politics to other situations in which most people end up feeling alienated," Tom replies. "For instance, I once read about workers on the Ford assembly line in the early 1980s who had the lowest morale in their industry. Predictably, Ford cars were at that time notorious for poor quality. So the managers at one plant tried an experiment. They installed a switch at every workstation that let any employee stop the whole assembly line. If a worker spotted a defect in any car, he could stop the line to fix the problem. Until then, only foremen could halt the line, which they rarely did. With the new switches in place, though, employees began stopping the line more than twenty times a day. Most of the halts lasted less than thirty seconds. Employee morale sky-rocketed. Car quality soared along with it. Ford sales soon took off."

"That's a powerful story," says Cassie, "but what is the connection to politics?"

"It's clear to me," says Jeffrey. "Each voter today is like a worker on the old Ford assembly line without any control over what's happening in front of him. Sure, he can flip any lever he wants, but what difference does it make? It doesn't. Unlike each European voter who gets a representative who shares his or her own political philosophy, a typical American voter cannot get a representa-tive who shares his or her strongest beliefs. Naturally, most of us feel power-less. Naturally, we react with despair. So most of us want to put politics out of our minds."

"Okay, I can see the point," says Cassie. "But can you make it less ab-stract?"

"Sure. I can make it very concrete," Jeffrey says. "Imagine someone who takes time out from work and family to learn what politicians are doing. Does all that time and effort improve his odds of getting a representative he can believe in?"

"Not really," Cassie admits.

"Someone who puts in that much effort is likely to end up feeling even more frustrated, even more upset about politics," says Jeffrey. "Of course, most people shun political life. It's like I said. The current system crushes the aver-age American's interest in politics."

"You've backed up that conclusion, awful as it is," says Tom.

"Even if he has," says Cassie, "people nowadays expect most Americans to be politically asleep. No one will do much about it."

"We've *got* to do something about it," says Tom.

"Yes," says Jeffrey. "If we don't, this country has had it."

"Give me a break," says Cassie. "That's so extreme."

"Really?" asks Jeffrey. "If most voters continue to feel helpless and continue to ignore what's happening on Capitol Hill, what's to stop Congress from steering the U.S. over a cliff, from ruining everything that makes this country great?"

"This country does seem to be headed downhill—on many fronts," says Tom.

"And we're going off the rails mainly because voters feel powerless to stop it," says Jeffrey. "Just give me a week to prove that's the prime reason."

"Sure. I want to see what you come up with. Who knows? You may uncover something that will shake up even Cassie."

Jeffrey nods at Tom, looks at Cassie intently, and heads out the door. By the time he reaches his office and sinks into his chair, he starts to worry. Maybe this time he's taken on too big a challenge. So he calls his favorite professor from graduate school, a man who served four terms in Congress.

When Jeffrey explains what he's trying to prove, the professor responds, "That's a very dark picture of a world I thought I knew. To convince me, to convince most people, you'd need plenty of ammunition. You'd need to do a lot of research."

"Whatever it takes," says Jeffrey. "Where do I start?"

8

While Most of Us Sleep,
Congress Does Its Worst

On the morning Jeffrey is to present his findings, he walks into Tom's office and sees Cassie chatting with a tall teenager wearing a Boston Red Sox baseball cap. "This is my son Ryan," says Tom. "He's visiting for a few days. When he gets back home, he's going to give his civics class a report on how Capitol Hill really works."

"What are you going to say?" asks Jeffrey.

"That this place needs an extreme makeover. But I know that my dad will figure out what to do here. He always figures things out."

"A walking campaign spot if I ever saw one," says Cassie.

"His mother would never allow it," says Tom, shaking his head. "She regrets letting *me* get involved in politics." Tom then says to his son, "Speaking of Mom, you said you'd meet her for lunch. You know she likes to eat early. Here's the address."

"Okay. I'm outta here. I'll let you guys fix this place."

Tom turns to Jeffrey, "What do we most need to fix?"

"Much more than I thought," says Jeffrey. "This time, I'd almost prefer that Cassie prove me wrong."

"Glad to oblige, Jeff. What do you think you've uncovered?"

"Let's start with two statistics that you often cite. First, most voters can't even name their member of Congress. Second, over 80 percent of voters have no idea what their representative is doing."

"Okay. Both are true."

"Well," says Jeffrey, "since most voters have no clue what their representative is up to, he can sell them out. Which most lawmakers do. On a regular basis."

"That's a helluva charge," says Tom.

"It's gotten to be a habit with him," says Cassie. "Everywhere he looks, he sees the system as broken." She turns to Jeffrey to ask, "How can you back up that broad an indictment?"

"For openers, one of the savviest lawmakers ever has publicly admitted—albeit indirectly—that the members of Congress make major policy decisions without considering their voters' welfare. It happened when the House was drafting a bill that would free banks, insurance companies, and brokerage firms from some long-standing restrictions. So the bill would have impacted nearly every household. The House Speaker at the time, Newt Gingrich, backed a version that would help insurance companies take business away from banks. He justified his stand to a reporter by saying: 'In the typical town, there is one bank president and 130 independent insurance agents. . . . Our freshman congressmen [can't] vote against independent insurance agents and hope to survive.'"

"A reasonable conclusion," says Cassie.

"Okay," says Jeffrey. "But notice that Gingrich never mentioned the 600,000 residents of each district who outnumber insurance agents more than 100 to 1. How come?"

"Because most people knew nothing about that bill, whereas bankers and insurance salesmen knew plenty," Cassie responds.

"Exactly," says Jeffrey. "And the same holds true on nearly every bill: The vast majority of voters have no clue what their representative is up to, while a few powerful people know very well. So the typical lawmaker caters to the powerful, knowing he'll get away with it."

"Maybe on obscure issues like that banking measure," says Cassie, "but not on subjects that the public pays attention to."

"On every issue," says Jeffrey. "Take the hottest topic of 1998, President Clinton's impeachment. Who on Capitol Hill based his or her decision on what he thought was best for his constituents or best for the country, for that matter?"

"Nearly everyone here acted out of pure partisanship," says Cassie. "You know that."

"The word 'partisanship' doesn't explain what each member of Congress was thinking."

"And you can figure out what went through peoples' heads?"

"You could figure it out, too," Jeffrey replies. "Each Republican incumbent calculated: 'Most citizens won't vote. And most who vote will have no idea what I've done in office. But if I vote for impeachment, the most right-wing citizens in my district will know for sure, so they'll vote for me in force at the next election, giving me a big margin of victory.'"

Tom turns to Cassie and asks, "Do you buy that?"

"More or less."

"And Democrats thought about it the same way," says Jeffrey. "They knew that if they backed Clinton to the hilt, the most liberal citizens in their districts would back them to the hilt. Meanwhile, most other people wouldn't even show up on Election Day. Both sides got it right: 98 percent of Republican incumbents and 98 percent of Democratic incumbents won reelection that year. Both parties won big by counting on most voters to be asleep."

"That strategy sure didn't work in 2006," says Tom.

"It worked fine for the 94 percent of incumbents who kept their seats that year," says Jeffrey. "And as for the small bloc of voters who helped unseat the other 6 percent, look what it took to stir most of them up: a war in Iraq that has strained our military to the breaking point, created far more terrorists than it's neutralized, decimated our standing in the world, and cost us a fortune."

"At least the 2006 election showed that if voters are provoked enough, they will punish the party they hold responsible," says Tom.

"Is that how you want this place to work? That to wake voters up, Congress has to contribute to a national catastrophe?"

"Of course not," says Tom. "But you still haven't convinced me that most of what goes wrong here stems from voter inertia."

"I have more evidence. Just look at how extreme Capitol Hill has become. Nearly every think tank that evaluates Congress has concluded that about 90 percent of lawmakers are pushing either hard left or hard right agendas. Yet over 40 percent of voters call themselves moderates. So how did the folks on Capitol Hill end up so much more extreme than the American people?"

"The state legislatures are at fault," Cassie interjects. "They draw each congressional district so it includes either a solid majority of Republican voters or a solid majority of Democratic voters. That's how Congress became so extreme."

"Nearly every pundit explains it that way," says Jeffrey, "but it doesn't add up. Let me show you. Take any lopsided district, say one that's 50 percent Republicans, with the rest split evenly among Democrats and independents. Is that skewed enough for you?"

"What's your point?" Cassie asks.

"Well, suppose the Republicans in this district nominated a moderate to run for Congress. Nearly all Republican voters would prefer him to the Democratic candidate. Some independents would too. So the moderate Republican should win a majority of the district's votes—easily. Right?"

"Yeah."

"But if the Republicans nominated a staunch ideologue, he should do worse. After all, he would turn off most independent voters, nearly all Democratic voters, and even some Republicans. So the ideologue could easily get less than 50 percent of the district's votes."

"I'm starting to see your point," Cassie admits.

"It's simple. Moderates should win consistently, while ideologues should lose about half the time. But in fact, ideologues win 90 percent of the seats. How do you account for that?"

Without waiting for Cassie to reply, Jeffrey turns to Tom. "The explanation is that less than 50 percent of district residents vote, and the vast majority who vote hardly care who wins. So the surest way for a candidate to win is to stir some sizable minority to vote in unusually large numbers. What better target than zealots from his or her own party? And as long as most people don't vote, that's how things will stay: most candidates will cater to zealots, who will thereby decide nearly every race."

"All you're saying is that the voters who care the most have the biggest impact on our elections," Cassie responds. "What's the harm in that?"

"The harm is that with the vast majority of voters inert, Congress can sell the vast majority of us out—with impunity—which it does," Jeffrey replies. "Congress has repeatedly shafted 99 percent of the American people."

"You have gone over the edge," says Cassie.

"Really?" asks Jeffrey. "How do you explain that Congress takes money out of every citizen's pocket and hands it to some of the most successful people? For example, the average farmer has *twice* the net worth of a typical household, yet the government gives farmers $45 billion a year in subsidies and indirect payments. Seventy percent of that money goes to farmers earning over $100,000 a year. And it's the average household that pays for those handouts—to the tune of $430 a year in higher grocery bills and taxes. So why do we take money from ordinary folks to subsidize people who do far better than most?"

"To preserve farming as a way of life," says Cassie.

"Bull," says Jeffrey. "Farms fail at one-sixth the rate of other businesses."

"Well, then, by subsidizing farmers, we don't have to rely on other countries for food," says Cassie.

"More hogwash," Jeffrey replies. "The *only* crops we subsidize are those that the world grows in the largest quantities—such as rice, corn, cotton, soybeans, and sugar. And many countries produce those crops far more cheaply than we do. So if we eliminated our subsidies, those countries could supply some of our needs at lower cost than we pay now. Every American consumer would end up saving money."

"At least subsidies help preserve American jobs," says Cassie.

"Another big lie," says Jeffrey. "Developing countries such as Brazil and India are retaliating for our farm subsidies by maintaining high tariffs on our manufactured goods. So U.S. businesses lose billions in sales. Farm subsidies thus *reduce* American jobs."

"Are you done?" Cassie asks.

"Not quite. Our farm programs also increase world poverty because farmers in poor countries can't compete with us. After all, our farmers get fat subsidies that let them sell crops for less than they cost to produce. One last point: Congress gives our most prosperous farmers more money than we spend on foreign aid. In effect, we devote more tax dollars to programs that keep people in poverty than to programs that lift them out of poverty. It's demented."

"Are you saying that our subsidies harm *everyone* but a small segment of farmers?" Tom asks.

"Absolutely," says Jeffrey. "And notice what makes all of that harm possible. It's that every lawmaker knows the vast majority of his voters have no idea how much of *their* money he's handing to the most successful farmers."

Tom turns to Cassie, "I think Jeffrey is right on this."

"Okay," says Cassie, her shoulders sagging. "But it's just one piece of legislation out of thousands."

"The same forces are at work on every piece of legislation," says Jeffrey. "The loud and the powerful get what they want. The public interest hardly counts."

"That's ridiculous," says Cassie. "What about all the environmental legislation of the 1970s. You favored that stuff big time."

"Those bills passed because environmental groups recruited millions of members, raised tons of money, and led massive Earth Day demonstrations. Yes, I believe that legislation served the public interest. But it didn't pass *because* of the public interest. It passed because well-funded lobbying groups made so much noise."

"I admit that Congress often appeases the groups that raise the biggest fuss," says Cassie. "But that doesn't mean that most bills harm everyone else."

"Congress has power over every aspect of our lives: our economy, our health, our security, you name it. If lawmakers use all that power with little regard for how it affects most of us, then of course they do harm, lots of it."

"That's too harsh for me to buy into," says Tom.

"Then, look at the tax code, some of the nation's most important legislation," says Jeffrey. "Nearly every provision is a gift to some powerful lobby at everyone else's expense."

"To put together any bill, lawmakers have to satisfy various interest groups," Cassie replies. "Making deals is the only way this place can work."

"Backroom deals would be fine if *most* people benefited from them," Jeffrey says. "But typically, most of us give while a powerful few get. For instance, every tax break that Congress gives to some powerful interest group ends up reducing government revenue. That means lawmakers have to tax everyone else more heavily. So, a few groups reap a fortune, while the rest of us get shafted."

"Even if all of your allegations about Congress are true," says Tom, "I still believe that *some* of my colleagues want to do the right thing."

"How many of your colleagues do the right thing if it means risking their seats?"

"If you put it that way, not many."

"The number is tiny," says Jeffrey. "Over the last five elections, 97 percent of incumbents from both parties have won reelection, most by huge margins. Were they just lucky?"

"Luck has nothing to do with it," Tom admits. "I see how far my colleagues go to maintain their big margins of victory."

"And each of your colleagues knows that very few voters have any idea of what he or she is doing. So if they do the right thing, it gains them nothing."

"I still don't believe that my colleagues *intend* to do harm," says Tom.

"Most of all, they intend to keep their jobs," Jeffrey replies. "And the surest way for any lawmaker to hang onto his seat is to cater to powerful interest groups, even if it's at everyone else's expense. Your colleagues thereby cause a lot of harm, which they get away with—because most voters let them."

"That's some ugly picture," says Tom. "It's almost surprising the country has survived."

"Give me fifteen more minutes. I can show that voter inertia threatens our survival."

"Melodrama on top of everything else," says Cassie. "Must you?"

"I'm just giving the facts, ma'am," Jeffrey says.

"The picture he's painting is so dark," Cassie says to Tom. "Do you think there's any way out of all this?"

"We can work our way out of the current mess," says Tom, "once we understand exactly what it is."

"Okay. But before he hits us with more doom and gloom, can we take a break?"

"Good idea," says Tom. "Let's meet back here in half an hour."

9

Does the Current System Threaten Our Survival?

"All right," Tom says to Jeffrey. "I see your point that voters are so disengaged that Congress gets away with horrendous decisions. You also said that our survival was at risk. And I confess that several issues keep me up at night. But first, I'd like to hear your list."

"Let's start with Medicare," says Jeffrey. "It'll bankrupt this country. To meet the program's commitments, its trustees admit that they would need $70 trillion in their coffers *now*. That's more than the net assets of every man, woman, and child in America. The government has, in effect, promised more Medicare benefits than our entire economy could deliver."

"For sure," says Tom. "That's worried me since long before I got this job."

"Yet," says Jeffrey, "in 2003, Congress saddled Medicare with even more commitments by covering prescription drugs. That hiked Medicare's deficit by $17 trillion, a move that both parties knew would push the country closer to bankruptcy. In fact, Democratic Senator John Breaux warned his colleagues that the 2003 bill was like 'throwing lead weights onto a sinking ship,' while Republican Senator Don Nickles cautioned that the bill was 'building another deck on top of' a 'very unstable house.' So why did Congress make such a fiscally insane decision?"

"Because seniors love those benefits," says Cassie.

"But what about everyone else?" asks Jeffrey. "Don't most people under fifty realize that by the time they retire, Medicare will implode? So they'll never receive the benefits they've paid for, the benefits that go to retirees today."

"Many people realize it," Cassie replies.

"What do they do about it?" asks Jeffrey.

"Not much."

"That's the problem. Most Americans under fifty don't vote. And most who do vote keep reelecting incumbents who've helped Medicare head down the tubes. So most lawmakers feel free to keep nudging us toward bankruptcy."

"I'm afraid," says Tom, "that we'll have a financial meltdown long before Medicare implodes. After all, Congress has been spending money so recklessly that we've had to borrow trillions of dollars from other countries. Someday, they'll want to be paid back. Where's that money going to come from? It's going to get ugly."

"Unfortunately," says Jeffrey, "voters keep reelecting incumbents who spend recklessly, so they will keep right on spending."

"You've made your point," says Cassie.

"Does that mean you agree that voter inertia threatens our survival?" asks Jeffrey.

"Financially, perhaps," Cassie responds. "Is that it?"

"No. I have two more stories that should trouble you," says Jeffrey. "First, you know as well as anyone that we buy 60 percent of our oil from other countries, some of which hate us, some of which finance terrorist groups bent on our destruction. In effect, we bankroll our worst enemies. And that huge pile of cash we spend overseas for oil, over $500 billion a year, is sapping our economy. On top of that, by using twice as much oil per person as the rest of the industrialized world, we generate more carbon dioxide per capita than any other nation, CO_2 that's heating up our planet. In my lifetime, that extra heat will scorch our Farm Belt, devastate our Gulf Coast with many hurricanes as brutal as Katrina was in 2005, and raise the sea level enough to flood our coastal cities."

"You're assuming that human activity is the main cause of global warming," says Cassie. "Many people disagree. They say nature itself is the biggest cause. And even scientists who say that we are at fault admit that they're guessing about how severe the consequences will be."

"Suppose we're only part of the problem and suppose that scientists' estimates are off," says Jeffrey. "Say the chance of a global catastrophe is only 50 percent. Isn't that ominous enough that we should take some steps to prevent it? Besides, our economy and our national security depend on reducing our addiction to foreign oil. And we can reduce it. For each of our energy problems, there are practical solutions.* So why have American politicians not enacted them?"

"Because," says Tom, "to cut our oil consumption enough to make a real difference, we'd have to alter our lifestyles more than most Americans want to. So most politicians are afraid to act."

"That's the explanation most people accept," says Jeffrey, "but it's only a small part of the story. After all, if we used less oil, the vast majority of us would be safer, richer, and healthier. That is surely worth some inconvenience to us. So why don't lawmakers make that case to their voters?"

"What's your explanation?" asks Tom.

"Every representative knows that most of his voters pay zero attention to him. So if he tackled our energy problems, it wouldn't benefit him. Whereas, if he sidesteps those problems, he knows he'll get reelected. And he's right. Voters keep reelecting incumbents who've let our energy problems grow worse."

"You think we can wake voters up?" asks Tom.

"There must be ways to get voters to think seriously about the issues that directly impact their lives," says Jeffrey. "They have so much at stake."

"All right, I buy that," says Tom.

"I don't," says Cassie. "And I don't buy that voter inertia causes as much harm as Jeffrey claims."

"I expected that," says Jeffrey. "So I saved my grimmest story for last. You'll see that voters consistently let politicians risk all our necks."

"Let's hear it," says Tom.

"Okay. To begin with, everyone on Capitol Hill knows that terrorists are trying to buy nuclear weapons in Russia because those nukes are so poorly guarded. Fortunately, despite all our differences with Russia, they have as little interest as we do in allowing lunatics to get their hands on nukes. So Russia has agreed to safeguard those weapons more rigorously, if we'll bear much of the cost. Unfortunately, Congress won't spend what the experts say it would take to do the job right."

"How much are we talking about?" Tom asks.

"Five to ten billion dollars a year. We spend a mere fraction of that. Meanwhile, Congress spends many times that ten billion dollars each year on pork barrel projects such as bridges that few people will use and museums that hardly anyone will visit."

---

* Appendix VI.

"The folks in this town have such deranged priorities," says Tom.

"But in this town," says Jeffrey, "deranged priorities make perfect sense. Because every lawmaker knows that pork for his district will win him some votes, whereas his decisions that really matter probably won't. After all, most of his voters have no clue about those decisions. So, the typical lawmaker makes them a low priority. As a result, terrorists may someday get their hands on a stolen Russian nuke that they could use on a U.S. city."

"I knew we were in trouble," says Tom. "But I never understood just how much."

Cassie grimaces.

"One last point," Jeffrey adds. "To halt a *potential* nuclear weapons program—one that turned out never to have existed—we've waged a war in Iraq that's cost over $600 billion, killed or maimed tens of thousands of Americans, killed or maimed hundreds of thousands of Iraqis, and alienated most of the world. Yet, without spilling one drop of blood, without offending a single ally, and without spending a fortune, we could be keeping thousands of nukes, which we *know* exist in Russia, out of dangerous hands. How could Congress make those two decisions—simultaneously? Because every incumbent knows that how well he makes critical decisions has little effect on whether he keeps his seat. He can make disastrous mistakes and the odds still remain over fifteen to one that his voters will reelect him."

"We can't go on like this," says Tom.

"What can anyone do about it?" asks Cassie.

"We have to fire voters up," says Tom. "We have to engage the vast majority of them in political life, really engage them."

"Never happen," says Cassie.

"Sure it can," says Jeffrey. "The last time we met, we saw why most voters are disengaged. A typical voter today can't get a representative who shares his or her own political values. That's why most voters ignore what their member of Congress is up to."

"Those are just the facts of life," says Cassie.

"They don't have to be," says Jeffrey. "What if we reorganized our elections so that each voter *does* end up with a representative who shares his or her political beliefs?"

"You're dreaming."

"We have to create that kind of bond between each American and his or her representative. Everyone would then have a damn good reason to pay attention to what their member of Congress was doing."

"Oh, to be young again and believe in Camelot."

"I'm being practical. Politicians will do what's right *only* if most Americans keep a close eye on them."

"Maybe so," says Cassie, "but what you're proposing can't be done."

"I'm not convinced of that," says Tom.

"But Jeffrey wants to make a change on a scale we've never tried before."

"American politics has changed plenty over time," says Jeffrey. "We abolished slavery. We . . ."

"But have there been shifts like the one you're suggesting?" Cassie interjects. "When have we ever changed the basic relationship between each representative and her constituents?"

"That could be a problem," says Tom. "To get people behind a change this big, we may need to show them that something like it has been done before."

"Don't you agree that the current setup is leading us to disaster?" asks Jeffrey. "That our survival is on the line?"

"Yes," says Tom, "but to go as far from the current setup as you want, we need more ammunition."

"All right," says Jeffrey. "Let me see what I can dig up." He stands. "What we need, I'm going to find."

10

Big Changes Can Happen

When Jeffrey walks into Tom's office nine days later, Tom is talking to Cassie about his weekend trips home for the next month. He is nodding slowly, with a dour expression on his face. "Thanks for putting this together," Tom says to Cassie. Spotting Jeffrey, Tom's face brightens. He asks, "What have you found this time?"

"It turns out that our elections have changed a lot over time," Jeffrey replies. "Within the last hundred years, women, minorities, and eighteen-year-olds have gotten the right to vote. Plus all of us have gotten the right to vote for U.S. senators. Originally, the state legislatures chose them."

"Big deal," says Cassie. "Those kinds of changes don't mean that the change *you* want can actually happen."

"But the change I want did happen—sort of—in the early 1900s in twenty-two U.S. cities. In New York, Cincinnati, Sacramento, and nineteen other places, voters were so fed up with local corruption that they converted their city councils to proportional representation."

"What?" says Cassie, furrowing her brow.

"Really?" asks Tom. "And if I remember correctly, with proportional representation, each voter is represented by his or her chosen party."

"Exactly," says Jeffrey.

"How come I've never heard of those cities having such different elections?" Cassie asks.

"Probably because all those cities, except Cambridge, Massachusetts, repealed the change. They went back to more traditional election methods."

"Aha!" Cassie exclaims. "So proportional representation bombed. Why then should we care about it now?"

"It proves that the *kind* of change we need now is doable," says Jeffrey.

"It also proves that when people are angry enough, they act," says Tom. "And people today are plenty angry."

"Not angry enough to push for something that's failed in the past," says Cassie.

"We just need to look at *why* proportional representation failed," says Jeffrey. "That would help us figure out an election process that really works."

"Why did all those cities give up on proportional representation?" Tom asks.

"It has one huge disadvantage, as I see it," says Jeffrey. "Each citizen is represented by a bloc of legislators, not an individual. So a typical citizen can't point to a specific person as his or her representative."

"Why does that matter?" Cassie asks.

"Whenever government screws up, a typical voter can't single out a particular lawmaker to hold responsible," Jeffrey replies.

"Sounds like a sweeping generalization," says Cassie. "Your specialty."

"A generalization? Sure," says Jeffrey. "But it's accurate. If voters can't hold a politician's feet to the fire, he'll work for his own interests more than the public interest."

"That sort of makes sense," says Tom, "but I also agree with Cassie. You're oversimplifying a complex subject."

"Based on hard research," says Jeffrey. "I took a close look at proportional representation—the kind once used here and the kinds used in other countries." He pulls out some papers. "I've written up what I've found.* You'll see that my conclusions are right."

"We don't have the time to read about other election methods," says Cassie. "We still have a district to represent, constituents to serve, an office to run. Remember?"

"To solve all the problems we've discussed these past weeks," says Jeffrey, "we have to check out approaches that others have tried. We don't want to start from scratch."

---

* Appendix VII.

"But why should we buy your analysis?" asks Cassie. "You have an agenda."

"My only agenda is to find something that works," Jeffrey replies. "I don't want us to repeat mistakes that others have made. And I can prove that what other countries have done won't solve America's problems. Just answer one question. In *any* country, do politicians make the big decisions consistently better than they're made here?"

"That's such a subjective question," says Cassie. "I can't name any such country. But that doesn't prove there isn't one."

"I agree with all of that," Jeffrey says. "So I contacted people who would know if any place fits that description. I called the most prominent advocates for proportional representation in the United States. I asked them, 'Does any country do such a good job of governing that most Americans would consider switching to that country's system?'"

"What did they say?" asks Tom.

"No one gave me a straight answer. One high-profile advocate acknowledged: 'We need to come up with an answer.' But when I called him again today, he still drew a blank."

"All right," says Cassie. "So, the methods used elsewhere won't solve America's problems. I could have told you that. The U.S. has in many ways been the most successful country in the world. So, for all its flaws, our government has done a better job than others have."

"That may have been true once," says Jeffrey. "But for years, at least since 9/11, our government has been a disaster. The last time we met, you agreed that Congress is making decisions that threaten our economy, our environment, our very survival."

"I remember," says Cassie.

"So most Americans feel less safe, less confident about the future, less trusting in our government than at any other time in my life," says Jeffrey. "We've lost our way. Admit it."

"Suppose I do," says Cassie. "What can any of us do about it?"

"We can organize our elections far better than we do now," Jeffrey replies. "The Constitution gives the states and Congress almost complete freedom to design House elections. And we'd better take advantage of that flexibility soon. We need politicians who will craft real solutions to today's problems. Our survival depends on it."

"But the task you want to take on can't be done," says Cassie. "You just told us that all these election systems in all these countries don't work noticeably better than ours do."

"That just means we need to avoid their pitfalls. Like I said, proportional representation has a fatal flaw: a typical voter doesn't have a specific representative he or she can hold personally responsible."

"That insight, even if it's right, is not enough for you to figure out a system that will solve all the problems you've been moaning about," says Cassie.

"We can't just accept the status quo. We've got to do something."

"Well, gee," Cassie says, "why settle for the ideal election system? While you're at it, why don't you figure out how to create world peace and end global hunger?"

"The challenge is huge. I accept that," says Jeffrey. "But we have to look for something better than we've got."

"To do anything *useful*," says Cassie, "you would need some edge over all the people who've tackled this challenge before. You're smart, Jeffrey, but you're not smarter than all the political thinkers of the last two centuries."

"Hold on a minute," says Jeffrey, looking up into space. "Designers of election systems have focused mainly on allocating power among political parties."

"So what?" asks Cassie.

"What they haven't done is figure out how to motivate lawmakers in the right way. No election system to date has motivated politicians from all camps to work together developing practical solutions to tough problems."

"And you think you can do it better?" asks Cassie.

"By myself, of course not. So let's recruit an expert who knows how to motivate people to work together productively."

"A psychologist?" asks Cassie.

"Okay. Why not?"

"This place runs on raw political power, not hidden impulses or motives."

"Well, then, let's find someone who has experience coaxing political enemies to resolve their differences."

"Like who?"

"Someone like former Senator George Mitchell. He nudged the various factions in Northern Ireland to govern together after all the previous efforts to make peace had failed."

"You think that kind of expertise will enable you to design an election system better than anyone has to date?" asks Cassie.

"We won't know till we try," says Jeffrey.

"The stakes are so high that it would be worth the effort," says Tom. "If we brainstorm enough, who knows what we'll come up with. What do we have to lose?"

"A lot of precious time," Cassie replies. "We have seven months until your next election. That's the ball we have to keep our eyes on. Instead, Jeffrey wants to waste our time on a challenge that no one could meet."

"It sounds ambitious to me too," says Tom. "But I can't accept the way that Capitol Hill works now. I hate it. We've got to figure out something better."

"I understand why you feel that way," says Cassie. "But I don't think you can find what you're looking for."

"I've got to try."

"Okay," Cassie shrugs. "It's your office."

"I need you to take part."

"What for?" asks Cassie. "In these sessions, I've just served as Jeffrey's foil while he tears apart everything about Congress."

"Listen," says Tom. "Every objection you've raised up to now has made sense to me. If Jeffrey hadn't answered your objections, I wouldn't have bought even half of what he said." Tom turns to Jeffrey, "Please don't take offense. You've done exactly what I've asked you to do. But we also need the hard-nosed reality testing that Cassie is so good at."

Jeffrey nods.

"Fine," says Cassie. "So, what do you want from me now?"

"I'll recruit a world-class peacemaker or mediator to brainstorm with us. We'll try to figure out how to coax lawmakers from the various camps to resolve the problems they mostly fight over now. I want you to join us. I want you to contribute every objection, doubt, and idea that you have."

"O . . . kay," says Cassie.

"I promise you," says Tom, "something good will come from our efforts."

Cassie nods, but she looks doubtful and unhappy.

Later, in her office, Cassie calls her husband: "How could I have let these two dreamers run rings around me time after time? They're lost in fantasy.

They could never navigate Capitol Hill on their own. I'm the real pro here. Yet the two of them have made me look inept."

"No one could make you look inept, hon."

"I appreciate that vote of confidence, but you haven't been at these sessions. The thing is, once Jeffrey gets an idea in his head, he digs and digs and digs until he unearths facts to back up his pie-in-the-sky conclusions."

"If you can't beat 'em, join 'em. You do research better than anyone I know."

"Well, I'm not going to let Jeffrey show me up again. But how do I top him? He and Hennessey are determined to cook up an election system that will turn the barracudas around here into saints. It's absurd."

"If you want to outdo Jeffrey and wow Hennessey, become an expert on election methods. Who knows what you'll come up with?"

"Those are the words that Hennessey used."

"If you want to impress him and outdo Jeffrey, that's how to do it: learn more about the subject than either of them."

"What a drag. But I guess you're right. I'm going to spin Jeffrey around like he's never been spun. But first, I need a break from this town. This weekend, let's go away—the shore, New York, you pick it."

"Sounds good to me."

Feeling better, Cassie wonders where to start her research.

Part III:
How to Get Politicians
We Can Believe In

11

Make Each Representative Accountable . . . for Real

When Tom walks into the offices of Creations Unlimited, five blocks from Capitol Hill, Sidney Falk is waiting for him in the reception area, reading a newspaper. Sidney's wire-rimmed glasses, windblown hair, and beard streaked with gray remind Tom of a typical professor. Yet Tom knows that Sidney often works far from a classroom, mediating political disputes, from local feuds to international treaties. In their phone conversation three days earlier, Tom felt a personal connection that he sensed was mutual.

Sidney greets Tom with a smile and a warm hello, adding, "I thought that meeting in a place like this would help us all move beyond traditional thinking. A friend of mine runs this outfit. Let me show you what we call the brainstorming room."

Tom follows Sidney into a room with chairs arranged in a circle, no table, and whiteboards on the walls. "This setting is fine," says Tom. "But my two staff members still may not give up their usual roles. They both have strong wills. And they spar a lot."

"We just need to channel that energy in the right direction."

"I hope we can. They know they can't solve this puzzle on their own. But I suspect that they also don't want an outsider to find the magic bullet. They have a lot invested in this."

"I don't have any magic bullets. The puzzle you're trying to solve is so big. . . . "

"Ah, here they are," Tom interjects.

Cassie and Jeffrey walk into the room, arguing. When they spot Sidney, they stop. Tom introduces them.

"When your boss first called," says Sidney, "I thought that one of my colleagues was playing a joke. They've all heard me agonize over why Congress makes such bad decisions. When I found out the call was for real, I was delighted. Thanks for inviting me. To make sure I'm in sync with all of you, would someone recap for me exactly what you want to accomplish today and what you'd like me to contribute."

"Ambitious as it sounds," says Tom, "we want to motivate the opposing camps on Capitol Hill to resolve America's urgent problems instead of fighting over them. We thought that your experience in refereeing political conflicts could help."

Sidney leans forward. "Well, as a mediator, I've seen long-standing enemies work out practical solutions on energy policy, Social Security, even abortion. But those opponents weren't elected officials."

"Congress never has that kind of success," says Tom. "So it would help us to know what motivated the adversaries you've worked with to collaborate with one another."

"They were at an impasse," says Sidney. "Everyone was frustrated—until some leaders in each camp realized that the most realistic way to make progress for their *own* cause was to sit down with their opponents and try to work out a deal."

"How civilized of them," says Cassie. "It must have taken more than that, though. Politicians can fight over an issue for decades, yet still refuse to work with their opponents."

"Each advocate I've known," says Sidney, "has had many people, sometimes thousands, pressuring him or her to get something done."

"My constituents make all kinds of demands on me," says Tom. "Those pressures drive me crazy. They often *stop* me from acting. I feel like a character in a cartoon, my head swiveling round and round as dozens of people shout at me, each saying something different."

"In the cases I've seen," says Sidney, "each advocate was in sync with his own group. An environmental leader, for instance, may speak for millions of environmentalists. A corporate CEO may speak for thousands of executives in his industry. So, the representatives I've known have *wanted* to meet their own group's demands. And the most practical way to get anywhere was to sit down with their opponents."

"Well, politics doesn't work that way," says Cassie. "The voters in a district sometimes rally around a cause that their local member of Congress fights for. But that doesn't guarantee results. On the contrary, lawmakers who fight the hardest for their own agendas can create the worst deadlocks."

"Hmm," says Sidney. "The advocates I've worked with have had a good sense of how their supporters were thinking. Each one was also confident that his supporters trusted him. He knew that if he negotiated a deal that made sense to him, he could explain it to his own camp and nearly everyone would listen to him make his case."

"What I hear you saying is that the 'right relationship' is all it takes," says Cassie. "Sounds a bit simplistic."

"The relationship is the most important piece," says Sidney. "Take an everyday conflict, say, a labor union struggling with a company. Typically, both the union rep and the management spokesperson have many people on their backs demanding results. So, the two negotiators roll up their sleeves, determined to work out a deal, which they usually do. Each representative then explains the pact to his or her own side with words like: 'This contract isn't exactly what we set out to get, but it's better than our alternatives. Here's how it stacks up. . . .' And since each spokesperson has, as you put it, the right relationship with his or her own people, they listen."

"Imagine, then," says Jeffrey, "if each legislator had that kind of relationship with his or her constituents. Imagine if they all shared his political values. Of course he'd want to strike deals that advanced those values. And whenever he struck a deal that made sense to him, he could explain to his own people how it would serve their shared agenda."

"Ever since you wrote that memo about James Madison, you've pushed the idea of each legislator speaking for citizens who share his or her political outlook," says Cassie. "You then planted the idea of our meeting with Sidney, who is portraying the same kind of relationship. Are we supposed to think that's a coincidence?"

"Call it whatever you like," says Jeffrey. "It makes perfect sense. Madison took part in many political negotiations, so he apparently understood what made them work."

"Okay," says Cassie. "Now, what do we do with these insights?"

"It's clear what we need to do," says Jeffrey. "If we want Congress to re-solve the issues it can't cope with now, each lawmaker has to represent a group of people who share similar values. Voters would then put consistent pressure on their representative to advance their cause. He'd have every reason to follow through. And, to get anywhere, he'd *have* to negotiate with opponents."

"Nice fantasy," says Cassie. "But do you have any *practical* suggestions for how to pull it off?"

"I'm working on it," says Jeffrey.

"I didn't expect you to have the answer," says Cassie. "Practicality has never been your strong suit."

"And what of any practical use do you have to contribute?" Jeffrey fires back.

"Well," says Cassie, pursing her lips, "I knew that to do anything useful today, you'd need to come down to earth. I had a hard time picturing that. So last week, *I* scoured the Web for information about election methods. I waded through tons of stuff—technical, polemical, all kinds. I even read your memo on the subject.* It was a fine summary, but it left out many details. Letting ev-erything percolate, I eventually saw just how to create the bond between each representative and her constituents that you've been hyperventilating about for months."

"You've been sandbagging us," says Jeffrey. "All morning you've sounded skeptical—as usual. Yet you had a solution in mind the whole time."

"Yes," she grins. "For months you've been broadcasting where you wanted us to go."

"She's right," Tom says to Jeffrey. "You've been on this horse since my first week here." Tom turns to Cassie, "You've had your fun. Now, I want to hear your grand scheme."

"It's not a grand scheme," says Cassie. "Just a little scenario that shows how to fulfill Jeffrey's dream of forging a strong connection between each law-maker and her constituents."

Jeffrey taps out a drum roll on his clipboard. "Okay, let's hear it."

---

* Appendix VII.

Cassie stares at Jeffrey for a moment and then says, "I'll start on a small scale. Suppose the residents of a tiny community want to elect a town council to represent them as ideally as you fantasize. So the whole town meets in a large hall. Each person who wants to be on the council hands out copies of his or her platform. After the townspeople question the candidates, the person running the meeting asks everyone present to gather around their favorite candidate. When everyone has gotten to their first choice, the moderator turns to the candidate with the smallest group around him and says, 'Joe, I see eighteen candidates running for the seven council seats. You have the fewest backers. So I'm going to ask you to drop out of the race. Then, would you and each of the five people gathered around you please make a second choice.' When each of those six people get to their second choices, the moderator turns to the next candidate with the fewest backers and asks her to drop out. She and each of her supporters go to their next choices. This process continues until seven candidates are left to fill the seven council seats."

"I get it," Jeffrey says. "Each person in this town would end up with a representative close to him politically."

"Closer than under any other election method now in use," says Cassie. "Plus each council member would know her constituents' concerns better than would a representative elected by other methods."

"Nice," says Sidney. "Still, each council member would need to stay in touch with her supporters to explain what she was up to."

"That's easy," says Cassie. "Each council member could ask her constituents to write down their names and addresses, including e-mail addresses. She could then send her constituents regular reports."

"Fine," says Sidney. "That way, each council member could explain any deals she made."

"Sounds good in theory," says Tom. "But each council member would almost immediately start to worry about the *next* election. I know. That concern would overshadow everything else. What happens then?"

"Long before the election," says Cassie, "each council member would wonder: 'Next time, my voters could again have eighteen or so candidates to choose from. So how will I entice my current voters to pick me as their *first* choice?' The obvious answer: 'I'll need to convince them that I've delivered more valuable results than any of the seventeen or so other candidates would.'"

"How could he ever convince them of that?" asks Tom.

"To produce the most useful results," says Sidney, "a representative would *have* to negotiate creative pacts with the rest of the council."

"Wait a minute," says Tom. "Wouldn't each council member find it easier to please his voters by saying he'd stood up for them, by proclaiming that he hadn't given an inch?"

"Do workers choose union leaders who provoke strikes?" asks Sidney. "It's very rare. Most workers want union leaders who negotiate good contracts. So if each voter could freely choose a representative, why would most voters pick someone who produced mostly angry rhetoric? It makes no sense. Most voters would want someone who produced solid results."

"This sounds too good to be true," says Tom. "You're predicting that each person elected this way would behave the *opposite* from how politicians act now."

"But the situation *would* be the opposite of the one now," Cassie replies. "Each council member would know that *all* the people she represented had signed up for her platform. So if she struck any deals that made sense to her, she could explain it to her voters."

"And every voter would be in a situation opposite of the one now," Jeffrey says. "Most people today can't possibly get a representative on their own wavelength. So most people don't vote, or they vote knowing little about the candidates. But if each voter had as many choices as Cassie is proposing, why would a voter choose a representative who just called his opponents colorful names? Voters would surely prefer a spokesperson who produced concrete results."

"Okay, I see how the situation would differ from the one I'm in now," says Tom. Then, turning to Cassie, he asks "How, though, does your proposal differ from proportional representation?"

"With existing proportional systems, a representative doesn't have specific constituents on her back demanding results from her personally," says Cassie.

"Ah, I remember."

"With my setup, though, each council member would have many citizens holding her feet to the fire. To assuage all those people, each council member would want to report progress on the important issues. And to have anything to report, she'd have to strike productive deals."

"In a small town, where everyone knew one another, I can see that happening," says Tom. "But it's a stretch to imagine the same result in a community with millions of people."

"Sure. So let me show you how any city can create a council that works the way I just described. It just requires organizing elections in the right way."

"You amaze me," says Jeffrey. "Until today, whenever I proposed a change, you mocked it. Now, you want to redo every town and city charter. You've flipped 180 degrees. Whose brain has been transplanted into that body? Where did the real Cassie go?"

"I'm right here," she laughs. "I still wonder how much of this we can actually implement. But I said I'd do my part. And I don't do anything halfway."

"That's for sure."

"Can we get back to the subject at hand?" asks Tom. "I want to hear how a real election can produce this incredible scenario that you just spun out."

"Sure," says Cassie. "Suppose a city wants to elect a council that works just like the one we've described. It takes four steps. First, all the candidates for all the seats compete in one combined election. That's just what the small town did, right?"

Tom nods.

"Second," says Cassie, "on Election Day, each voter chooses which candidate is his or her first choice. That's the same as in the small town. Yes?"

Tom nods again.

"But each voter's first choice may not win a seat," says Cassie. "So, each voter also needs to pick a second choice. And, in case that candidate doesn't win, the voter picks a third choice, and so on."

"This is starting to sound complicated," Tom says.

"It isn't though," Cassie responds. "To make all those choices, each voter gets what's called a 'preferential ballot.' It's simple. When filled out, it looks like this:

BALLOT FOR CITY COUNCIL

Please choose which of the candidates listed below is your first choice, and put a "1" in the box next to his or her name.

Then choose which candidate is your second choice, and put a "2" in the box next to his or her name.

And so on. You may rank as many candidates as you like.

Robert Adams	[ ]
Shana Pierce	[3]
Robert Green	[1]
Lois Kaplan	[ ]
Thomas Washington	[ ]
Sylvia Hernandez	[2]
Steven Gross	[ ]
Arthur Houseman	[4]
Cynthia Gray	[ ]
Phillip Kowalski	[ ]

"Does everyone see that this ballot mimics the small town's election?" asks Cassie.

"Sure," says Tom. "Instead of each voter physically moving to his or her preferred candidates, each voter marks his or her choices on this ballot."

"Exactly," says Cassie. "Then, the people running the election count citizens' first-choice votes. Or computers can do that job."

"And the candidate who draws the fewest first-choice votes is out of the running. Right?" asks Jeffrey.

"Yes," says Cassie. "Say Robert Green draws the fewest votes. Every person who voted for Green as their first choice then has their vote count for their second choice."

"And once those votes are added to each remaining candidate's tally, the next candidate with the fewest votes is eliminated, right?" asks Jeffrey.

"Sure," says Cassie. "And then, everyone who voted for that candidate has their vote count for their next choice. And so on."

"I see," says Tom. "The lowest-drawing candidates are dropped one by one. Eventually, the number of candidates left will equal the number of council seats."

"You got it," says Cassie. "You can see exactly what this vote counting looks like with this table I put together." She hands each of them a page titled: "How to Count Preferential Ballots."

How to Count Preferential Ballots

Suppose that each voter could rank all the candidates running for city council: a 1st choice, 2nd, 3rd, and so on. Say the initial vote tally was:

VOTES FOR CITY COUNCIL: First Tally

1ST CHOICE VOTES:

Phillip Kowalski	24,643
Lois Kaplan	18,733
Steven Gross	16,308
Robert Adams	15,644
Sylvia Hernandez	14,673
Shana Pierce	12,812
Arthur Houseman	10,793
Cynthia Gray	9,623
Thomas Washington	8,901
Robert Green	6,481

The candidate with fewest votes—in this case, Robert Green—would be out of the running. Each vote for Green then goes to the candidate listed next on that voter's ballot. Adding those votes to each candidate's total might produce the following tally:

VOTES FOR CITY COUNCIL: Second Tally

	1ST CHOICE VOTES:	2ND CHOICE VOTES: (FROM GREEN'S VOTERS)	TOTAL:
Phillip Kowalski	24,643	884	25,527
Lois Kaplan	18,733	654	19,387
Robert Adams	15,644	967	16,611
Steven Gross	16,308	213	16,521
Sylvia Hernandez	14,673	839	15,512
Shana Pierce	12,812	612	13,424
Arthur Houseman	10,793	752	11,545
Thomas Washington	8,901	1,186	10,087
Cynthia Gray	9,623	374	9,997

Then, the next candidate with the fewest votes is eliminated. In this case, it's Cynthia Gray. All the people who voted for her have their votes count for their next choices. This process is repeated until the number of candidates left equals the number of seats.

"With this process, I see that each voter gets a council member on his or her own political wavelength," says Sidney. "But how does each council member stay in contact with his voters?"

"Good question," says Cassie, thinking. "How about this? The day after the election, every voter is mailed a card that lists the election winners. Each voter is asked, but not required, to check off the name of the person they want to represent them. The voter then mails the card to that winner. Each representative thereby receives her constituents' names and addresses. She can then send them regular reports about her work on the council."

"I send out tons of mail," says Tom. "Most people throw it into the garbage—unread."

"With this new election process, though," says Cassie, "your voters would look at politics in much the same way you do. So most of them would care what you had to say far more than the bulk of your voters care now."

"And," says Jeffrey, "if you and your voters had a similar outlook, you could explain your decisions on the serious issues. You wouldn't have to duck controversial subjects."

"In fact," says Sidney, "if all of your constituents shared your political values, you'd want to report as much progress to them on the important issues as you could."

"This scenario sounds like it came from a different planet than the one I live on," says Tom. "You all really think that changing elections could alter how every lawmaker thinks and acts? I'd like to believe it."

"What doesn't ring true to you?" asks Cassie.

"For openers, you've assumed that many candidates will compete in each election. How can you be sure that will happen?"

"Why not let anyone who collects enough signatures on a petition run for office?" asks Jeffrey.

"Good idea," says Cassie. "On top of that, each party would want to nominate *several* candidates to run in the general election. After all, with one election for *all* the council seats, each party would want to field many candidates in order to maximize its odds of winning seats."

"Okay," says Tom. "If the nominating process was opened up that much, I suppose elections would be more competitive than ever."

"But you still have doubts," says Cassie.

"Yes," says Tom. "Voters will always know incumbents' names better than the challengers'. So, won't incumbents always be natural favorites to win again?"

"Only in the kind of elections we have now," says Jeffrey. "After all, today, each of us can vote for only one person. So if I vote for an underdog, what happens? Nothing. Nada. Zilch. The frontrunner still wins. My vote has no effect. Naturally, most people don't vote, and most who do vote just choose the name they know: the incumbent. Incumbents thereby keep their seats no matter what kind of job they do."

"That much I'm aware of," says Tom.

"With a preferential ballot, though," says Jeffrey, "if an incumbent disappoints his voters, they can pick new faces as their first few choices. And even if a voter's first few choices lose, his vote will go to other candidates he can live with. So any voter with a preferential ballot has a good reason to think hard about which candidates he or she really prefers."

"I think I follow that," says Tom.

"Let's make it concrete," says Cassie. "Sidney, suppose your town used a preferential ballot to elect its local council. Say your favorite candidate wins a seat. But once elected, he gets little done. He blames opponents for getting in his way. So before the next election, you check out other candidates. Remember, you'd have a ballot that looks like this:

BALLOT FOR CITY COUNCIL

Please choose which of the candidates listed below is your first choice, and put a "1" in the box next to his or her name. Then choose which candidate is your second choice, and put a "2" next to his or her name. And so on. You may rank as many candidates as you like.

Robert Adams	[ ]
Shana Pierce	[ ]
Robert Green	[ ]
Lois Kaplan	[ ]
Thomas Washington	[ ]
Sylvia Hernandez	[ ]
Steven Gross	[ ]
Arthur Houseman	[ ]
Cynthia Gray	[ ]
Phillip Kowalski	[ ]

"Suppose Bob Adams is the guy you voted for last time. And say that two other candidates—Cynthia Gray and Stephen Gross—make a good case that they'd achieve more of what you want for the town than Adams has. What would you do?" asks Cassie.

"I guess I'd vote for Gray and Gross first and second," says Sidney.

"But Gray and Gross may lose," says Cassie.

"So I suppose I'd pick Adams as my third choice, just in case."

Jeffrey turns to Tom, "The point is that with a preferential ballot, each voter can vote his true feelings. Anyone who disapproves of the incumbents can pick challengers ahead of them."

"I get it," says Tom.

"The bottom line," says Cassie, "is that in a preferential election, if an incumbent doesn't deliver results, most of his voters will pick other candidates ahead of him. To stay in office, an incumbent has to convince his voters that he's done better work than would the other candidates."

"What constitutes better work?" asks Tom.

"What voters want," says Jeffrey. "Progress on the important issues."

"I'd like to believe you're right," says Tom. "I'd like to believe that this process will work as well as all of you seem to think. But so many questions occur to me. I need a break to mull all of this over."

"I think we could all use a break," says Sidney.

Outside, Tom walks toward the Mall. It's filled with office workers eating lunch, tourists, businessmen, hot dog vendors, park rangers, and joggers. A man snaps a photograph of what appears to be his wife and two daughters with the Capitol dome in the background. Tom imagines them flipping through the pictures around their kitchen table back home, showing friends, saying, "Yeah, that's the Capitol behind us, where they screw everything up." Two men in shirtsleeves pass by, with government ID badges hanging around their necks. Tom overhears a snippet of conversation. "The answer is simple," the taller one says. "We just stall it out for another couple of weeks."

Tom shakes his head, takes out his cell phone, and calls his wife. He tells her about the meeting. "I feel like I'm strolling through the Twilight Zone. Everyone in this town assumes that the culture is set in stone, that no one can change how Capitol Hill works. Then Cassie, who's clung to the status quo as tightly as anyone, comes up with this incredible idea for turning politics upside down and inside out. I'd like to believe that kind of progress is possible, but I don't know if it is."

"What's your alternative, sweetie?" asks Kelley.

"My alternative is to keep watching this town operate in a way that makes me sick," says Tom. "It doesn't seem to concern anyone in power that the two parties keep eviscerating each other. I think the country is more torn apart than at any time since the Civil War."

"Not to mention that many of us out in the real world are scared," says Kelley. "Most people I know are afraid that the country is headed downhill."

"They have good reasons to feel that way. I can't just watch it happen. I won't just stand on the sidelines while this country goes to hell."

"I know you won't. You didn't give up a job you loved just to collect a bigger paycheck. You went to Washington to make a difference."

"I guess that means I go back to the meeting and do whatever I have to do to convince myself that Cassie's idea will work—or not."

"Go for it."

12

How Ideologically Diverse Do We Want Our Politicians to Be?

When Tom re-enters the brainstorming room, the others turn toward him. Cassie wolfs down the last bite of a sandwich. Sidney signs off on his cell phone. Jeffrey snaps his laptop shut.

"I really want your idea to work," Tom says. "So let's get beyond the theory. Tell me how your plan would affect *us*. How would you organize House elections?"

"Like my earlier examples," says Cassie. "Each election would be for *several* representatives at the same time. The easiest way to set that up would be to merge the existing congressional districts into larger ones—so each ends up with several lawmakers. To pick those legislators, each district would need lots of candidates across the political spectrum. On Election Day, each voter would get a preferential ballot. She could then choose the candidates she favored first, second, third, and so on. The candidates drawing the fewest votes would be eliminated one by one—until the number left equaled the number of seats to be filled."

"How many representatives would each district have?" asks Tom.

"If each district had three lawmakers, then nearly every American could get a representative on their third of the spectrum," Cassie replies. "That would be a huge improvement over today."

"Why be so timid?" Jeffrey exclaims. "Why not eliminate districts entirely? Let each state have one statewide election for all its House members. That would be so much better."

"In some ways," Cassie admits. "But statewide elections would also entail big risks."

"Both of you, please slow down," Tom says. "I need you to lay out the pros and cons of the various choices."

"Sure," says Cassie. "Let's start by supposing that each district had three lawmakers. Then, to win a seat, a candidate would have to draw about a third of the voters. That means candidates on the fringes couldn't win. The winners would nearly all come from the three main camps—conservative, liberal, and moderate. In fact, a typical district would end up having one representative on the right, one on the left, and one in the center. So every American would feel far better represented than now."

"Not every American," says Jeffrey. "In some districts, one of the main camps wouldn't be represented at all. Take a place like Manhattan. If it were one three-member district, it would likely elect two liberals and a centrist. The conservatives would be shut out."

"Manhattan is far more politically skewed than most places," says Cassie. "You're the one who buried us in statistics about how nearly every district is diverse by incomes, jobs, etc. So don't distract us with an unusual case. My point remains: In a typical district with three lawmakers, the vast majority of voters would end up with a representative on their third of the spectrum. So every voter would be better represented than now, when all of us in a district have to share one legislator."

"Okay, but many people would still be dissatisfied," Jeffrey replies. "For instance, most Republicans who backed John McCain in the 2008 presidential primaries wouldn't be content if someone like a Mike Huckabee ended up being their district's representative on the right. Meanwhile, many who backed Huckabee wouldn't be satisfied with someone like McCain. But if districts were eliminated, then the representatives in a typical state—which has nine House seats—could include the equivalent of a McCain, a Huckabee, a Mitt Romney, a Rudy Giuliani, a Ron Paul, a Mike Bloomberg, a Barack Obama, a Hillary Clinton, *and* a John Edwards. You gotta admit that nearly every voter would be delighted to have a representative among that field."

"But that's not how it would play out," Cassie replies. "Because in addition to the mainstream candidates, some extremists would also end up in Congress. After all, if a typical state held one preferential election for its nine House seats, an extremist would need to draw just one-ninth of the voters to win. So in most states, a socialist would likely win, as would someone further on the militant right than we ever see now. Mainstream Americans would strenuously object. They don't want representatives in Congress who are more extreme than those we have in office now. That possibility alone would prompt many people to oppose this whole plan."

"Why let prevailing attitudes dictate what we propose?" asks Jeffrey. "People who you think are on the fringes have a right to be represented. Our goal should be to include every camp at the table."

"If you want to see this election process happen," says Cassie, "it has to be a change that most Americans can support. That's what I'm trying to deliver. So give me a break. Rein in your hunger for perfection. This country isn't going to take one huge leap into the unknown. We have to propose something practical."

"To justify all the work it will take, we also have to come up with something great," says Jeffrey. "Three reps per district doesn't cut it."

"That's ridiculous," says Cassie. "Even with three legislators per district, the tens of millions of voters dissatisfied with both the Republican and Democratic parties would turn to other parties, which would win many seats. That alone would be an historic change."

"Big deal," says Jeffrey. "Fifty percent of Americans say they'd like another major party."

"Which means that 50 percent wouldn't like it."

"Tough," says Jeffrey. "To make a big change, we have to rattle some cages."

"Not necessarily," says Cassie. "What if we proposed two-member districts? Republicans would likely win about half the seats. Democrats would probably win the rest. Even fans of the two-party system could live with that setup. I think I'll write up the case for that option."*

"Oh no," Jeffrey groans. "You started out with a great idea—by which nearly every voter ends up with a representative that he or she can believe in. Don't cripple your beautiful process by trying to preserve the worst parts of the current system. New parties would be a huge plus. Even for Republicans and Democrats. After all, the Republican Party now includes both the Christian right and libertarians, both internationalists and unilateralists, both laissez-faire capitalists and interventionists. Meanwhile, the Democratic Party tries to include everyone from socialists to centrists. Each party ends up battling with itself over nearly every issue."

---

* Appendix VIII.

"Having more parties in Congress would not end intra-party strife," says Cassie.

"True," says Jeffrey. "But with more parties, each one could frame a more consistent platform, an agenda that voters could actually grasp. So, more voters would identify with a party than do now."

"Where on the spectrum would new parties come from?" asks Tom.

"Since over 40 percent of Americans label themselves moderates, and most of them are dissatisfied with the two major parties, the new parties would mostly come from the center," says Jeffrey. "What's more, with the elections that Cassie is proposing, the House would roughly mirror the American people. So centrists would likely win about 40 percent of the seats, three times as many seats as they hold now."

"So the House would steer more toward the middle of the road," says Tom. "Sounds good to me."

"That scenario assumes that most citizens would vote by ideology," says Sidney.

"Three-quarters of American voters place themselves somewhere on the left-right spectrum," says Jeffrey. "Ideology does matter to most."

"But not to all," says Cassie. "So what? With these elections, even a person who didn't vote ideologically would get a representative to whom she felt a closer bond than she does now."

"But wouldn't that bond between each citizen and her representative be a lot stronger if each district had three representatives rather than if it had just two?" asks Jeffrey.

"Yes," says Cassie.

"So will you back off on two-member districts?"

"Three-member districts have a big advantage. I admit that."

"Thank goodness," says Jeffrey.

"Suppose I push for three representatives per district. Will you?" asks Cassie.

"I buy your argument that most people would object to statewide elections. But why just three reps per district? Why not four or five?" Jeffrey asks.

"Because having more than three would increase the risk that some representatives would fall outside the three main camps, which would increase the risk that many mainstream Americans would resist our whole plan," Cassie replies. "As things stand, we're proposing two huge changes: preferential ballots and multi-member districts. So let's restrain our ambitions to something that might actually happen. That's why I'm for three representatives per district. It's strictly for practical reasons."

"I can see the logic of it," Jeffrey says. "Okay. I'll go along—for now. But I still think this subject deserves more discussion."

Cassie laughs. "Fine. For now, can we all agree on three-member districts?"

"I can see that it's the most realistic alternative," says Tom.

Sidney nods.

"One thing, though," says Jeffrey. "What about states whose number of House seats isn't divisible by three? Massachusetts, for instance, has ten seats."

"Those states could have some two-member districts," says Cassie.

"No, no," says Jeffrey. "In a two-member district, at least one major group can't be represented: either the liberals, the conservatives, or the moderates. That stinks. So for states whose seats aren't a multiple of three, let's propose an occasional four-member district."

"You are a pain in the butt," says Cassie.

"What's your problem? In those few four-member districts, *one* rep *could* fall outside the mainstream. All the rest would be your standard liberals, moderates, and conservatives."

"All right, already," says Cassie. "I can live with that."

"Great," says Jeffrey.

"You realize, though, that some states have only one House seat," says Cassie. "Some have only two. Those states will have to have one- or two-member districts."

"Bummer."

"But those states could still use preferential voting," says Cassie. "Each voter could pick a new face as his or her first choice. So incumbents would feel far more pressure to perform than they do now."

"That would be an improvement," says Tom. "Are there any other steps we need to work out?"

"I think we've covered the basics," says Cassie.

"Okay," says Tom. "So recap the whole thing for me in a way that we could easily explain to anyone."

Cassie starts ticking the points off on her fingers. "One: Existing congressional districts would be merged into larger ones, so that most districts would end up with three representatives. I'll draw up a table of exactly what size districts each state would have.*

"Two: Candidates would get on the ballot one of two ways—either by obtaining enough signatures on a petition or by winning enough votes in a party primary.

"Three: Each voter would get a preferential ballot.

"Four: When ballots were counted, the lowest-drawing candidates would be dropped from contention, one by one, until the number of candidates left equaled the number of seats in that district.

"Five: Each voter would be mailed a card listing the winners in the district. Each voter could then mail the card back to the representative he or she preferred. Each rep would thus have a list of her constituents. So she could report to them regularly."

"And you all agree that this proposal is better than the system we have now?" Tom asks.

"I think so," says Cassie.

"In every way," says Jeffrey.

"I need to think about it some more," says Sidney. "So far, I see only advantages."

"That strikes me as too good to be true," says Tom. "Every idea has some drawbacks. And a change this big is bound to have effects we haven't thought of yet. So let's try to imagine what could go wrong with this rosy scenario. Let's take a break while each of us thinks about that."

Cassie nods. Sidney stands up and arches his back. Jeffrey looks out the window, deep in thought. He then picks up Cassie's handout about how to count preferential ballots and wanders into the hall.

Tom is sure they'll think of flaws. He hopes that whatever problems they find they can also fix.

---

* Appendix IX.

13

Cementing the Bond Between Citizens and Lawmakers

Jeffrey walks back into the room shaking his head, frowning. "I see something that'll derail this whole idea."

"Let's hear it," says Tom, grimacing.

"With the elections we've proposed, each winner would draw a very different number of voters," says Jeffrey. "In a district that's electing three lawmakers, for instance, one winner might attract 500,000 voters, another 300,000, and the other 200,000. Yet every representative would have equal power in Congress. That wouldn't be fair to the people who backed the most popular winner."

"Oh no," Cassie groans.

Jeffrey continues, "It would be like going back to the days when a typical urban district had about 500,000 people, while a typical rural district had less than half that number, yet every district got one representative with the same clout. Each urban voter thus had less than half the clout of a typical rural voter. The Supreme Court banned that practice more than forty years ago. Every person's vote has to count equally."

"I knew it," says Tom. "There had to be a glitch."

"Sorry, boss," says Cassie. "I thought I'd covered all the angles."

"I hate being the one to torpedo this idea," says Jeffrey.

"I have a question," says Sidney. "Inside the legislature, couldn't each lawmaker get voting power based on the number of people he or she represented? So if the winners in a district got 500,000, 300,000, and 200,000 votes, that could be each lawmaker's relative voting power."

"With all due respect," says Cassie, "that's a weird idea."

"I appreciate your trying, though," Tom adds.

Jeffrey tilts his head to think for a moment. "Hold on," he says. "Each *state* gets votes in the House proportional to the number of people who live there. Why, then, shouldn't each *lawmaker* get votes proportional to the number of people who back him?"

"Because," says Cassie, "the idea sounds bizarre."

"If we want Congress to work substantially better than it does now, to actually solve the problems it mostly bungles now, we *have* to do something different than we do now," says Jeffrey. "You've figured out most of what we need to do to get there. You've figured out how to give each voter a real representative. But to finish the job, to reap the benefits of your plan, it looks like we need to add Sidney's idea."

"Sidney's scheme might have benefits, but it would also have drawbacks," says Cassie. "For one thing, the most powerful lawmakers could run roughshod over all the others."

"I don't see how," says Jeffrey. "After all, the House has 435 members, which means the average lawmaker represents less than 1/400th of the U.S. population. So if a winner got double the average, he'd still represent less than 1/200th of the population. Big deal. No small bloc could control the agenda. To pass any bill, at least 100 lawmakers would have to support it."

"In fact," says Sidney, "the legislators with the most voting power would likely wind up on different sides. They wouldn't form a united bloc. To pass any bill, its backers would still have to build a coalition from various camps. So negotiators who built the largest coalitions would wield the most influence, more influence than representatives with the most voting power."

"Okay," says Cassie. "What you're proposing might work. But your logical arguments won't prevent many people from fearing something this strange."

"The first time people saw a locomotive belching smoke, most were scared silly," says Jeffrey. "Yet when they saw the advantages of railroads, people demanded more of them."

"I suppose," Cassie allows.

"Well, Sidney's idea has huge advantages, too," says Jeffrey. "Most people would love to have a representative who works for what they believe and reports to them regularly. But anyone who wants that strong a bond has to accept that each lawmaker will appeal to a different number of voters. It's inevitable. So, each lawmaker has to have power based on the number of his voters."

"That logic is hard to argue with," says Tom. "But does the Constitution allow lawmakers to have unequal voting power?"

Jeffrey closes his eyes to think.

"Has he memorized the Constitution?" asks Sidney.

"Every word," says Cassie, arching her eyebrows. "Buy him a couple of beers and he'll also recite the Declaration of Independence and the Gettysburg Address."

Jeffrey opens his eyes, "The Constitution says that each senator shall have one vote," he smiles and adds, "but has no such clause about representatives."

"How'd that happen?" asks Tom.

"To induce the smaller states to endorse the Constitution, the framers had to give each state equal power in the Senate. So every state got two senators and every senator got one vote. In the House, though, the framers wanted to distribute power by population, which they did. The idea of representatives *within* a state having different voting power just never came up. But I doubt that the founders would object because they wanted to allocate power in the House by population. They also wanted to create a strong bond between each representative and his constituents."

"I'd like to believe this idea could work," says Tom.

"It would work better than today's setup," Jeffrey says. "If each representative had power based on the number of his backers, every American would know that his or her vote truly counts. Each of us would also know that everyone we recruited to vote for our favorite candidate would add to his clout in Congress. So, most people would want to spread the word about their chosen candidate. Americans would participate in politics more than ever."

"Sounds almost too good to be true," says Tom.

"Something else just hit me," Jeffrey adds. "Sidney's proposal has another big advantage. State legislators would no longer have a reason to draw districts with artificial boundaries."

"What do you mean?" asks Tom.

"These days," says Jeffrey, "nearly every state legislature draws each district to benefit someone or some group, often to favor one party over the other.

But if each group got power based on its numbers, a legislature couldn't give any group substantially more power than its fair share. It couldn't deprive any large group of power."

"Get serious," says Cassie. "State legislators will always find ways to draw districts to suit their own political ends."

"They'll always try," says Jeffrey, "but if lawmakers had power in proportion to their popular support, the distribution of power wouldn't depend on how districts were drawn anywhere near as much as it does now. On paper, I can prove that for sure."*

"Okay," says Cassie. "I buy that. But despite all the advantages of Sidney's idea, it's still too far out for Congress to consider."

"An idea like this won't *start* in Congress," says Jeffrey. "It'll start at the grass roots. Plenty of communities are disgusted enough with their local school board or town council to try our whole package *if* folks thought it would give them a political process they could believe in."

"That I can accept," says Cassie. "But if a small school board or town council, say with five members, used your proportional voting scheme, one member could conceivably obtain majority power."

"So," says Jeffrey, "any small town that adopts this process would need to enlarge its council to, say, nine or more members. With that many seats to fill, half the town would never agree on one candidate. The people in any community have opinions all over the lot."

"But on a nine-member council, two or three candidates might garner majority power," says Cassie."

"When that happened," says Jeffrey, "it would matter only if the most powerful lawmakers were all on the same side, which would occur rarely. And even if a few representatives had majority power, that would be fairer than the alternative. After all, in any American community today, does each group have its fair share of power?"

"I don't see how that's possible," Tom says.

"Well, I guess it isn't," says Jeffrey. "But any community could get much closer to that ideal by adopting an election system that gives each group power based on its size. It would certainly be the fairest option."

"In that case," says Tom, "who could argue against it?"

---

* Appendix X.

"Anyone who doesn't like a big change from what they're used to," answers Cassie.

"Let me ask you something," says Tom. "On the day you got your first computer, how did you feel about it?"

"I wanted to smash it," says Cassie.

"And now?"

"I can't live without it. . . . Okay, I see your point."

"Something else just occurred to me," says Tom. "Remember how much you doubted that we could come up with a better election system than anyone else has to date? You were right to be skeptical. It was wildly ambitious. Look what it took. We had to step outside the box."

"Way outside," Cassie says.

"Fair enough," says Tom. "In fact, I wonder if anyone has tried elections even remotely like these?"

"I'll bet that somewhere individual lawmakers have different voting power," says Jeffrey. "May I do a quick Google search?"

"Go ahead," says Tom.

Jeffrey flips open his laptop and types away. "Sure enough. In upstate New York, the Livingston County legislature gives each member voting power based on the number of voters in his district. And I'll bet that other places use that feature."

"That helps, that it's actually used somewhere," says Tom. "What about preferential ballots?"

"They're used in several places, too," Jeffrey replies. "And in several ways. First, there's the 'single transferable vote,' the proportional system that twenty-two U.S. cities tried many years ago and all but one repealed. As I said when we last met, I think that system failed because a typical voter couldn't point to a specific person as his or her representative."

"I remember," says Tom. "All the same, some people will expect us to explain in detail how our plan differs from a preferential system that's been tried and failed before."

"Okay," says Jeffrey. "But what those cities did is pretty convoluted, far more convoluted than what we have in mind. It would take a while to explain. I could write up a description of how it differs from what we want to do."*

---

* Appendix XI.

"Good," says Tom. "We may need that at some point. Does any other system use a preferential ballot?"

"Oh, yes," says Jeffrey, "there's 'instant runoff voting.' San Francisco began using it in 2004. Since then, Minneapolis and Oakland have adopted it, and other cities are considering it."

"How does it differ from our proposal?"

"An instant runoff produces only one winner."

"In that case," says Tom, "don't many voters end up opposing that one person who wins?"

"Yes," says Jeffrey. "But for elections that must produce one winner, such as for a mayor, a governor, and so on, preferential ballots are a big improvement over the elections that we use today. Because with a preferential ballot, every citizen can vote his or her true preferences and know that his vote will count. So citizens have a stronger incentive to vote and to think hard about whom to vote for. We should use preferential ballots in every election, presidential races, too."

"One revolution at a time," says Tom. "Right now we're trying to figure out how to fix legislative races, not mayoral or presidential ones."

"Sure," says Jeffrey. "Still, I'd like to write up the reasons for using preferential ballots in one-winner elections.* I'll do it on my own time."

"Fine," says Tom.

"Speaking of other election methods," says Cassie, "we need to give our new process a name. And let's not use a label as boring as 'single transferable vote' or 'instant runoff voting.'"

Jeffrey laughs.

"The name should convey that our process would connect lawmakers and citizens like never before," says Tom.

"Interconnected representation?" asks Cassie.

"That doesn't grab me," says Tom.

"How about 'personally accountable representation'?" asks Jeffrey.

"That's better," says Tom.

"Or 'personally accountable representatives'?" asks Cassie.

"Yes," says Tom. "That describes the people. I like it."

---

* Appendix XII.

"We'll need both names," says Cassie. "Sometimes, we'll need to describe the people; other times, the process."

"To me," says Jeffrey, "both names suggest that citizens stay on their representative's case—even between elections."

"I like both names," says Sidney.

"I guess that makes it unanimous," says Tom. "Okay. Cassie, would you write up a one-page description of 'personally accountable representatives.' Try to include everything that we've agreed to here."

She nods.

"And over the next few days," Tom continues, "let's think about how to get this idea off the ground."

"The first thing we'd better do," says Cassie, "is think of objections that people will raise and figure out how to answer them."

"Sounds right. Sidney, can you make it the same time next week?"

"I wouldn't miss it," he says.

Back in his own office, Tom calls his wife. "We had to add some bells and whistles to Cassie's plan. Overall, it would be a huge improvement over the current setup. All my constituents would back my political agenda. We'd have a real connection. I could push the issues that really matter to me. And all my colleagues would be in that same seat." Tom then goes into detail about how the new system would work.

"Sounds great," says Kelley. "How do you make it happen?"

"That part we haven't figured out yet," Tom says, laughing. "We saved that for another meeting. For sure, it would take years to bring about. But I'd have a cause I really believe in. Which is a helluva lot better than cringing at the prospect of going to the office each morning."

"Amen to that. So, what exactly do you do next?"

"Reality testing. I'm sure we'll be hit with tons of objections."

"You'll deal with them."

"I hope so. For now, I gotta get back to the mound of paper piled on my desk. Love you. I'll call you tonight."

As Tom leaves the office that evening, Cassie hands him a sheet of paper, saying, "When you have a chance, let me know what you think."

In the elevator, Tom sees that it's a two-page description of the new election process. As he begins to read it, a smile crosses his face.

PERSONALLY ACCOUNTABLE REPRESENTATION

Personally Accountable Representation (PAR) is a process by which each lawmaker becomes directly responsible to a group of citizens who all share his or her political outlook.

To create this relationship between each representative and his or her constituents requires the following steps:

1. The community schedules an election in which all the candidates compete for all the seats in one combined election, or they compete in districts that will have several representatives each.

2. Candidates get on the ballot by obtaining a sufficient number of voter signatures or by winning a party's nomination.

3. The local election board circulates basic information about all candidates to all potential voters.

4. On Election Day, each voter gets a "preferential ballot." Each voter can mark which candidate is his or her first choice, second choice, and so on.

5. When the ballots are counted, the candidate with the fewest first-choice votes is eliminated from the running. All the votes for that candidate go to his voters' second choices. Then, the next candidate with the fewest votes is eliminated. All the votes for him or her go to his or her voters' next choices. In this way, the lowest-drawing candidates are eliminated one by one.

6. Candidates are eliminated until the number remaining equals the number of seats to be filled.

7. The day after the election, every voter is mailed a card that lists the election winners. Each voter is asked (but not required) to check off the name of the winner that he or she prefers and to mail the card to that winner. Each representative thereby gets her constituents' names and addresses. So she can send her voters regular reports about what she is doing in the legislature.

8. Each lawmaker gets voting power proportional to the number of his or her voters.

PAR OFFERS THE FOLLOWING ADVANTAGES OVER OTHER ELECTION METHODS:

- Each voter gets a representative close to him or her politically, as close as is practical.
- Each citizen thus has the maximum incentive to scrutinize the candidates and to vote.
- Each lawmaker knows his or her constituents' political concerns better than under other methods.
- Each lawmaker knows that at the next election he or she will face intense competition for his seat.
- Each lawmaker thus feels far more pressure to produce useful results.
- Each lawmaker therefore has more incentive to reach agreements with opponents.
- Each lawmaker is in the best possible position to explain difficult decisions to his or her constituents—in terms they can accept.

14

Answering Skeptics

I n the days after the brainstorming session, Tom struggles to focus on his job. He really wants to work on the new election plan. He gets his chance at week's end, when Jeffrey drops off a memo. Seeing the subject, Tom tells his secretary to hold all calls and starts to read.

> **TO:** Rep. Tom Hennessey
> **FROM:** Jeffrey Lazlo
> **SUBJECT:** Handling Objections to Personally
> Accountable Representation

To prepare for our next session, Cassie and I asked friends and colleagues for their reactions to PAR. They raised many questions and doubts, nearly all of which Cassie and I were able to answer. So we thought you'd like to see our responses. They may come in handy when we pitch PAR to others.

The objection we heard most often was that average Americans are so politically disengaged that even PAR won't get them to participate more in political life. We responded with your story about Ford Motor Company workers given a switch to control their assembly line.*

---

* page 66.

Most people saw our point: if workers are given real choices, they put far more thought and effort into their jobs. From there it was easy to convince folks that voters given a real choice of who will represent them on the critical issues would put more thought and effort into that part of their lives.

Still, the objection kept popping up in other forms. So we found additional ways to answer it, which you'll see below.

We put all the material in a question-and-answer format. That way, readers can scan the questions and read just the replies that interest them.

One caveat: Until PAR is widely used, we can't prove that it will do all we say. Not yet. We can still make a strong case for it. We just need to point out to folks that under the current system, Congress has repeatedly proved itself incapable of making intelligent decisions on the important issues. Then we need to show that PAR would give both lawmakers and voters the incentives to make sound decisions, more so than any other reform that people are considering.

Most Americans are busy tending to their jobs, families, and homes. So will most of them ever take the time to keep closer track of politicians and the issues?

Americans spend an average of four hours a day watching television: sports, soap operas, sitcoms, and "reality shows" that have nothing to do with the reality of their own lives. People watch TV mostly to escape—in part from feeling helpless about matters that concern them. For instance, if you ask people on the street what issues they care about, most will talk passionately about something. Yet most people will also confess that they feel helpless to do anything about it.

With PAR, though, each person could choose a spokesperson for the issues that concern him or her most. Many Americans would thus invest more time and energy thinking about those issues and less time numbed out in front of a television.

There are so many big issues: taxes, health care, national security, education, trade, and so forth. Will voters ever keep track of how their legislator handles all of that?

If each of us could truly choose our representative, a typical voter would keep a closer eye on how his or her chosen representative handled the issues that impacted the voter the most. That alone would be a huge improvement over what goes on today.

Won't some voters, given more choices of candidates, feel overwhelmed?

Look inside any store, from a supermarket to a car dealership. Most Americans want choices. And with a preferential ballot, voters don't have to narrow their choice down to one candidate. Each voter can pick as many or as few candidates as he or she likes. Most people would find that task easy. Most people have a good sense of which candidates they prefer.

A typical voter today chooses between one Republican and one Democrat for each office. With PAR, though, voters would have ten or more candidates to choose from. How would voters sift through the information on that many candidates?

Each candidate could craft a brief statement of his or her basic philosophy—say, in fifty words or less. Those statements could then be sent to all registered voters. Each voter could read those brief statements to pick the candidates who most appealed to him. The voter could then look at those candidates' full platforms to decide which ones he or she prefers most.

How would voters get their hands on candidates' platforms?

In many communities, the local election board mails each registered voter the bios and platforms of all candidates. For House elections, the federal government could send to every American of voting age a guide to the candidates in their area. Plus, the Internet would have copious data about the candidates.

Some voters, given more choices, would surely make poor decisions. So wouldn't some PAR lawmakers be more incompetent than those we have now?

For that to happen, hundreds of thousands of voters in a district would have to choose the *same* incompetent candidate. Plus in a House of 435 members, a few troublemakers couldn't make much difference. To do serious harm, tens of millions of us would have to pick shady characters.

Even with PAR, wouldn't most candidates aim for the largest audience in their district? If so, most candidates would end up making similar pitches.

That outcome is unlikely because if any large segment of a district lacked a credible candidate, some people are bound to show up to fill the vacuum. For instance, in a particular district, suppose that no liberals with a track record had entered the race. That situation would surely prompt some politically active liberals to run for a seat.

Even with PAR, wouldn't politicians appeal to voters with superficial ads and slogans?

Vacuous ads and slogans work only for trivial products. For instance, ads for soap imply that it will improve your love life. A dubious claim, yet it helps sell soap because most consumers have no desire to investigate the various brands. It isn't worth the effort. So people tend to buy the brand that conveys the most sex appeal.

For important products, though, that strategy is far less effective. To advertise a home, for instance, no one describes a rundown shack as a mansion. Because to most people, their house is a big deal. Anyone buying a home checks it out carefully. So an ad for a house has to describe its true features—or the ad is a waste of money.

How does that apply to politics? *Today,* most people care about voting even *less* than their choice of soap. After all, everyone uses soap, but most people don't vote, except in presidential elections. And in congressional races, more than 80 percent of voters know nothing about the underlying product: the candidates. Most people just vote for the name they know best: the incumbent. If the incumbent doesn't run, voters are influenced by candidates' ads more than by their actual track records. It's clear why: a typical voter can't get a representative he believes in.

What if, instead, each of us could get a representative who championed what we truly cared about? Most of us would place a higher value on our votes. As much as on our homes? Probably not. But more than on our choice of soap. Most voters would want to know what the candidates intended to do in office—because those decisions would directly affect each voter's life. So, most libertarians wouldn't vote for a liberal even if she had a photogenic family and a catchy jingle. Most internationalists wouldn't vote for an isolationist even if he flashed a toothy smile. In a PAR world, substantive ads would be more effective than superficial ones.

Won't candidates always find it easier to sling mud than to explain a complex platform?

In an election in which more than two candidates have a realistic chance of winning, slinging mud is a dangerous strategy. Both the person throwing the mud and the person it's thrown at look bad. The mud mostly benefits other candidates. In a typical PAR election, ten or more candidates would compete on a preferential ballot. So anyone who tossed mud would be helping other candidates more than himself. After all, if some candidates dealt with the issues that voters cared about while others hurled insults, who would most voters pick as their first choices?

Challengers would still be trying to unseat incumbents. So wouldn't challengers still level all kinds of charges against incumbents?

No doubt. But to win, a challenger would have to show voters that he'd achieve more for them than the incumbent they'd favored in the last election. If a challenger strayed from the important issues to personal attacks, he'd just help other candidates.

To see how PAR candidates would likely compete, think back to when many contenders debated face-to-face before the first presidential primaries in 2008. Both parties' debates were civil and substantive. Most people watching were surprised. But in a contest in which many candidates have a chance to win, anyone who wants to win has to campaign on substance.

With PAR, each incumbent would know that his or her voters had supported his or her platform. And he or she could feed those voters a constant stream of information at government expense. So in every election, wouldn't incumbents still have a huge edge over challengers?

With PAR, voters would have many more candidates to choose from than they have today. Each voter would also have a preferential ballot and could easily rank challengers ahead of incumbents. So if any incumbent did a mediocre job, his or her voters would have real alternatives. Incumbents would therefore win reelection less often than they do today.

To attract the most voters with the least effort, wouldn't many candidates focus on the hottest issue at the time?

If most voters could get a representative who shared their basic political philosophy and thereby shared their views on many issues, why would anyone focus on only one subject? A typical person doesn't pick a car for its gas mileage alone, while ignoring its age, condition, cost, color, and brand. No one picks a home based on one feature alone. There are too many features that count. Likewise, Congress wrestles with many subjects that affect each person's life. So, if voters had a real choice, most wouldn't choose candidates based on one issue. They would choose candidates based on their overall outlook.

Liberals fight among themselves on issue after issue. So do conservatives. So do moderates. How, then, will any politician ever satisfy most of his or her voters?

Most people interested in politics have a favorite newspaper columnist whom they disagree with on some issues. Yet most readers stay loyal to their chosen pundit. Why? Because each columnist articulates a philosophy or way of thinking that appeals to his or her readers so strongly that they stay loyal, even though they disagree with some of his stands.

A PAR lawmaker would be in a similar position. Nearly all of his constituents would occupy his part of the political spectrum, so he could champion a set of values that nearly all of his voters supported. If he did that job well, he could keep his voters' loyalty—even though each voter might disagree with him on several issues.

With PAR, most voters would expect their representative to meet their political needs better than ever. So wouldn't many voters have high expectations that politicians couldn't satisfy?

Voters would learn what to expect. In real life, people often start out wanting the moon, but when they see what they can get, they become more realistic. When shopping for a car, how many folks expect to find a Rolls-Royce at a price they can afford? Not many. Likewise, as people became used to PAR, they'd figure out what politicians could reasonably deliver.

With PAR, what percent of voters would get their first choice?

If ten candidates competed for a district's three seats, the laws of probability predict that three of the candidates would typically win about 60 percent of the first-choice votes. Those three candidates would win most of the time, but not every time. So, a little less than 60 percent of voters would see their first choice win a seat. Most of the rest would get their second choice.

Wouldn't voters whose first choice didn't win end up disappointed?

To some extent, but PAR would give more voters the representative they wanted than would *any* other system. We can't do better than that.

If a PAR representative left office in the middle of a term, how would he or she be replaced?

Those voters who had identified him or her as their representative (by sending in a card after the original election) would get to vote for his or her replacement in a special election. That election would of course use a preferential ballot.

Wouldn't a typical PAR lawmaker cater to his or her voters' expectations more than shape those expectations?

In a House of 435 members, no lawmaker would have enough power to fulfill most of his voters' expectations. To achieve as much of their agenda as possible, he would have to work with other legislators on measures that served many competing interests. He'd then have to show his voters how that strategy benefited them. If they didn't buy his explanation, they'd boot him out of office. So to keep his job, a PAR lawmaker would need to shape his voters' expectations.

To find the best solutions requires top-notch research and analysis. Will politicians whose main skill is winning votes ever be up to that job?

Congress turns to staff members and outside experts for most research and analysis. In the current environment, though, most lawmakers have little interest in the best solutions, so they largely ignore the research and analysis. The best we can do is to give politicians the maximum incentive to seek out the best solutions. That is PAR's purpose.

Would PAR lawmakers ever advocate controversial ideas to their constituents?

A representative who has constituents on his or her own wavelength can show them how a controversial idea will serve their interests. For instance, if a company is in trouble, a union representative can show workers how they'd benefit by forgoing a wage hike and, instead, accepting bonuses based on profits. A PAR representative could likewise explain to her constituents how they could benefit from ideas they hadn't considered before. A pro-environment lawmaker, for instance, could explain to her voters the benefits of raising gasoline taxes while lowering income taxes the same amount: That combination would cut America's need for foreign oil, help clean up the air, and slow down global warming, yet cost the average family nothing.*

Though the idea would be controversial, the representative could prove to her voters that she was looking out for their interests more than candidates who didn't consider hiking gas taxes.

Aren't there simpler ways to fix American politics, such as redrawing congressional districts so that the typical one has roughly an equal number of Republicans and Democrats? In that case, independent voters would decide most congressional races. So many more moderates would win seats, substantially reducing the influence of ideological extremists.

That kind of change would not be sufficient to motivate most lawmakers to make sensible decisions on the hard issues. After all, as long as each lawmaker competes for his or her seat with one challenger from the other major party, every lawmaker will have a stronger incentive to bash the other party than to work with it. Furthermore, as long as one person represents each district, the vast majority of Americans will be unable to obtain a representative who shares their own political values. So, most Americans will remain alienated, uninformed, and uninterested in what their representative is doing. Therefore, the typical representative will have as little incentive to make hard decisions on the controversial issues as lawmakers do now.

Until the day comes that most Americans have a good reason to believe that their representative is on their side, most Americans will not trust their representative sufficiently to listen to him or her make a case for hard decisions. Therefore, very few lawmakers will make hard decisions. So, our most serious problems will continue to fester.

The bottom line is that simpler reforms are wholly inadequate for the challenges this country now faces.

---

* Appendix VI.

With PAR, wouldn't some districts elect at least one representative who advocated an agenda that most Americans would consider extreme?

Perhaps, but for any PAR lawmaker to accomplish anything, he or she would have to negotiate with other camps. Then he or she would have to explain to his voters how negotiating with opponents was the only practical way to advance their own cause. In effect, for a PAR representative to keep his or her job, he or she would need to become a voice of reason to his or her own voters.

If this scenario sounds far-fetched, just look at any successful negotiator: To close any deal, he or she has to prove to his or her own camp the value of cooperating with the other side or sides.

How would PAR affect the hold that lobbyists and interest groups have over politicians?

Politicians cater to lobbyists in order to get money with which to buy campaign advertising. And these days, nearly every candidate cares a great deal about the *amount* of advertising he or she can buy because most voters simply cast their ballots for the name they know best. With a lot of advertising, a candidate can pound his or her name into voters' heads. At the same time, more than 80 percent of voters don't know or care about the candidates' track records—including how much they've sold out to special interests. So a politician who takes lobbyists' money indiscriminately pays almost no price for it.

PAR would change that equation. Most voters could get a representative who shared their own values, so most would care plenty about the candidates' track records. And if each of us had a preferential ballot, anyone who thought that a candidate had sold him or her out would vote for other people. So a PAR politician who got too close to special interests would ruin his or her own career.

Even so, candidates could boost their odds of winning elections by buying more ads. So politicians will always be after money and therefore always prone to corruption. Will PAR address this problem?

To reduce the influence of money, the government could send each voter a booklet with the platforms and bios of all the candidates in his or her district. Each candidate could thereby get his or her basic message out regardless of how much money he or she had.

In addition, the government could send every household one DVD or videotape that contained a twenty-minute message from each candidate in the district who had agreed to cap his or her campaign spending at a preset amount.

This is just an option, though, not a key part of PAR. As we see it, lawmakers do their worst because most voters pay no attention to their lawmakers. So, most of all, we need to cure voter apathy, which PAR could do better than anything else people are considering.

If PAR's purpose is to create a stronger bond between each representative and his or her constituents, why not give each lawmaker half the number of constituents he or she has today?

That's a good option. But it would mean doubling the House's size to 870 members. To many people, that number would sound unwieldy. PAR already consists of three controversial ideas: preferential elections, multi-member districts, and proportional voting power. Adding a fourth point that sounds radical would just distract people from our main message.

How would PAR affect the media's coverage of politics?

The media cover topics that people care about. So if the average American cared what his or her representative was up to, print media and websites might keep track of what each lawmaker was doing. A group like C-SPAN might even start a cable channel on which each lawmaker was allocated time slots when voters could phone in to grill him. He or she would, in turn, get a chance to tell his story.

Wouldn't most PAR legislators still cave in to constituents' expectations? For instance, just about everyone wants higher Social Security and Medicare payments. So wouldn't PAR legislators shower voters with those benefits while trying to conceal the costs—just like today?

If voters today take the time to figure out how much government programs are costing them, what can they do about it? Not a thing. Nearly every voter is stuck with the district incumbent for as long as he or she wants to stay. So most voters lack a reason to find out what Congress is up to.

With PAR, though, each voter could get a representative who championed what the voter cared about. What voter would choose a lawmaker who spent the voter's tax dollars recklessly? Suppose, for instance, that incumbents kept handing out benefits to seniors while hiding the costs. With PAR elections, some candidates would surely show voters under fifty that they were paying for retirees' benefits that they themselves would never see. Voters who could truly choose a representative would have solid reasons to act on charges that they were being robbed.

PAR would thereby ignite a war between seniors and other generations. Do we want to stir up that kind of conflict?

An honest conflict between generations would serve the country more than what Congress is doing today: financially ruining future generations. Besides, conflicts between the generations can be resolved. In 1998, twenty-four advocates across the spectrum agreed unanimously on how to save Social Security in a way that would be fair to every age group. Lawmakers could do the same—if they were genuinely motivated to solve America's problems.

Cassie and I are still refining our answers to this question and a few others that people raised. We'll have more by the next meeting.

— JL

15

How America Could Reach Consensus

"Fran Sinclair got a hold of our two-page handout on Personally Accountable Representation," Tom says to Cassie, Jeffrey, and Sidney as they sit down in his office. "She stormed in here, saying that we were all nuts. Fortunately, your Q&A helped me defuse most of her criticisms. But she had a bunch left. So I invited her to join us today."

"What's her biggest objection?" asks Jeffrey.

Before Tom can answer, he sees Fran striding through the doorway, ramrod straight, looking as tough and imposing as ever. "Let me introduce you," he says to her. "This is Sidney Falk, the mediator I told you about. Cassie and Jeffrey you know."

"Yes. Roger Blake used to love their work. What he'd think now, I'd rather not say."

"I'm the one who steered them down the road we're on now," says Tom.

"A one-way road to nowhere," says Fran. "Even if PAR could change lawmakers' motivations as much as all of you to seem to think, that doesn't mean the House could work out the nation's differences on issues as nasty as Social Security and Medicare. What have you all been drinking?"

"For nearly every major issue," says Sidney, "I know of ideological adversaries who've crafted a real solution—one that would give each camp what it needs most."

"Sure, sure," says Fran. "Everyone thinks they can do better than us. Tell me, though, these groups that have concocted your grand schemes for fixing America's problems, how many members did they have?"

"Between ten and twenty-five."

"Satisfying twenty-five people is a lot easier than pleasing the 435 members we have here," says Fran. "And dealing with one divisive issue is a layup compared to our job of dealing with every national issue. None of the geniuses you've worked with has ever had to cope with the number of complex issues that every one of us has to deal with."

"So how do you manage that job?" asks Sidney.

"We hand the work out to committees. They write nearly every bill. Yet your description of PAR ignores that part of Congress. Which shows me that all of you are flying around in the stratosphere."

"Okay," says Sidney. "Bring me back to earth. Tell me how your committees operate."

"Party leaders assign all committee seats," Fran replies. "Most committee members want to stay in their leaders' good graces, so they push their party's platform. Usually, committees end up writing bills that toe the majority party line."

"Blatantly one-sided bills," Jeffrey interjects. "Or just as often, committees fight to a deadlock."

"That's how the real world works, son," says Fran.

"With all due respect, Congresswoman, that's how Capitol Hill works," Jeffrey says. "And now that you've brought up the subject, it occurs to me that congressional committees are organized just as dysfunctionally as our elections are."

"What are you talking about?" Fran asks.

"Wouldn't you agree that each lawmaker represents so many constituencies that she can't possibly satisfy them?"

"Yes. So what?"

"Each committee member faces that predicament several times over: As you just pointed out, nearly every committee member wants to placate her party leaders. She's also beholden to her biggest campaign contributors. Plus each committee member owes favors to various colleagues. And of course, she has to worry about her voters, at least those who are paying close attention to her. Every committee member thereby ends up speaking for an array of constituencies, each with a different agenda. So whatever a committee member does on a controversial issue can get her in hot water with some constituency she cares about. In that situation, what's the safest outcome? An impasse. That way, each committee member can at least say to all of her constituencies that she fought hard for their interests, but that other camps were intransigent."

"You're oversimplifying but not that far off the mark," says Fran. "Big deal. In a PAR House, each committee member would still have to deal with party leaders, colleagues, donors, and voters."

"Sure," says Jeffrey, "but each PAR lawmaker would be after the same goals as the vast majority of her voters. And those voters would be paying more attention to their representative than now. So a typical committee member would want most of all to advance the platform that her voters had signed up for. The only way to make progress on that platform would be to strike creative deals with other committee members."

"Even if everyone in a PAR House wanted to reach agreements, they'd still be overwhelmed with as many conflicts as we are now," Fran replies.

"If they organized their committees in the right way, they could resolve those conflicts," says Sidney.

"You don't give up, do you? On what do you base that sweeping claim?" Fran asks.

"It's based on the many adversaries I've seen strike productive agreements. For instance, in the mid-1990s, twenty-five top environmentalists, industrialists, and government officials met regularly to thrash out their differences over environmental policy—because that was the most practical way for each one to make progress for his or her own camp. They succeeded, eventually developing a long-range plan that addressed the major environmental questions of that time. The business members of this council then pitched the plan to corporate executives around the country. The environmental members sold it to fellow environmentalists. And the government officials sold it to other regulators. My point is that you can resolve any issue if you assemble the right representatives."

"What you call the right representatives might be easy to find on an issue like the environment, where the world divides into a few well-defined camps," says Fran. "But on *every* issue, do you think that 435 lawmakers could organize themselves into coherent camps and—then—that each camp could agree on its ideal spokesperson? If so, you're hallucinating."

"Ah, but PAR can organize *any* group of people into politically coherent camps," says Sidney. "PAR also enables each camp to pick the right spokesperson. That's the whole point."

"Son of a gun!" Tom exclaims. "The House itself could hold PAR elections."

"For what?" asks Fran.

"For each committee," says Tom. "Take Ways and Means. Each lawmaker who wanted a seat would write out his agenda on taxes and circulate it among all his colleagues. Each member of the House would then fill out a preferential ballot, picking which candidate for Ways and Means was his or her first choice, who was his second choice, and so on. The lowest-drawing candidates would be eliminated until we had a committee of, say, twenty-five members."

"Notice," says Sidney, "that this way every committee member would be representing a group of colleagues who were in synch with him or her on the subject of taxes. All of them would be counting on him personally to advance the cause they shared. And the only way he could advance that agenda would be to negotiate with representatives from other camps."

Fran looks hard at Sidney. "That setup *could* work. They could negotiate for real. But that doesn't mean they *would*."

"Let me ask you something," says Sidney. "If a committee chosen this way couldn't reach agreement on a major bill, would each bloc of lawmakers reelect the same representative?"

"I suppose not," Fran replies hesitantly.

"So you understand that if the House held PAR elections, for any committee member to keep his seat, he'd have to get things done. If he didn't, his colleagues would look for someone who could. So, each committee member would feel enormous pressure to reach agreement with his counterparts."

"In fact," adds Jeffrey, "the closer a committee came to consensus on a bill, the higher the odds that both the House and Senate would pass it intact. So nearly every committee member would want to reach consensus. Because that way, each one would know that the provisions he had negotiated—the provisions he and his allies cared about—would actually become law."

The room is silent, until Fran says, "That's quite a scenario. You may even be right. Too bad it'll never happen."

"Why not?" asks Tom.

"Because if we chose committees that way, party leaders would no longer control committee assignments. And they'd fight with everything they've got to keep that power."

"Sure," says Cassie, "but if a majority of lawmakers want to override their party leaders, they can. In the years you've been here, in both the 1970s and '90s, rank-and-file lawmakers rebelled against the old guard to make changes in House committees."

"But what you're all suggesting would constitute a much bigger challenge to party leaders than ever before," says Fran.

"Yes," says Cassie. "But lawmakers will always push for procedures that help them get reelected. Surely you agree with that?"

"Yes."

"So what committee structure do you think PAR lawmakers would adopt?" asks Cassie.

"Who knows?"

"A minute ago, you seemed to accept that our committee setup would enable Congress to put together practical agreements on the toughest issues. So wouldn't PAR lawmakers demand that setup?"

"That's such a hypothetical question," says Fran.

"You know more about how this place runs than anyone I know," says Cassie. "And your first reaction was that this arrangement would help Congress work out deals on really nasty issues."

"Look, I can see that your proposal might produce more agreements on those issues than other arrangements would. That's as far as I'd go."

"That's quite a statement coming from you," says Tom.

"Don't break out the champagne just yet," says Fran. "Your setup must have flaws. I just need to think about it more. For now, I've said what I have to say. It's time for me to leave."

After Fran is gone, Tom smiles with relief, "Good work, guys."

"But she didn't buy what we were selling," says Jeffrey.

"She never will. She'll never accept PAR," says Tom. "She does too well under the current arrangement. She'd sooner give up her first-born child. But you got as much out of her as you could. You really had her cornered."

"Yeah," says Cassie, smiling. "Sidney, that committee structure is a great idea."

"It came to me because of your insight about a preferential election," says Sidney.

"The four of us make a good team," says Cassie. "Even so, we'll encounter plenty of people around here who won't be convinced. One objection will definitely come up: Instead of two political parties battling for power in each committee, we're proposing that twenty-five different camps vie for influence on each committee. Some people will insist that arrangement would lead to gridlock even more often than now."

"That's easy to answer," says Jeffrey. "Congress gridlocks so often these days because the two parties compete for just about every seat. Naturally, incumbents from each party try to make the other one look awful. If they reach an impasse, each lawmaker can blame the other party—for being intransigent or extreme."

"That much is clear," says Cassie.

"In PAR elections, though," says Jeffrey, "liberal legislators would woo liberal voters. Centrists would court centrists. And so on. For the most part, lawmakers would *not* compete with candidates elsewhere on the spectrum. So why would lawmakers spend energy bashing colleagues elsewhere on the spectrum? In fact, any lawmaker who wanted to accomplish what his constituents had elected him for would have to build alliances. He would have to negotiate agreements. If instead, Congress gridlocked on an important issue, he would end up disappointing most of his voters. So they might not reelect him. In effect, gridlock could cost him his seat."

"That follows," says Tom. "But what about the other side of the Hill? The Senate might kill or maim every bill that a PAR House passed."

"That's a real risk," says Cassie. "Because to change Senate elections, we'd have to amend the Constitution. That's too big a challenge to contemplate—even for Jeffrey."

"We don't need to change Senate elections," says Jeffrey, "because whenever a PAR House passed an important bill, most members would want to rally their constituents behind it. So if the Senate blocked the measure, many voters would get angry and vote against the senators who were responsible. In effect, senators who'd stalled the bill could lose their seats."

"You really think that voters would become that more vigilant?' asks Cassie.

"If most voters had a representative they genuinely believed in, yes," Jeffrey replies.

"I buy that," says Tom. "Something else occurs to me: if a PAR House passed major legislation that most Americans supported, would senators sit still while the House got all the glory? No way. Most senators couldn't stand playing second fiddle to the House. They'd want at least as much public approval. And to produce equally good legislation, the Senate would have to reorganize its committees—so that its various factions could work out their differences."

"PAR committees alone would do the trick? Is that what you think?" Jeffrey asks. "Wouldn't that mean we don't need PAR elections?"

"We need PAR elections to draw voters wholeheartedly into the political process and to goad members of the House to do quality work," Tom replies. "That, in turn, would light a fire under the Senate."

"I get it," says Jeffrey.

"But we still haven't covered all the bases," says Tom. "How would a PAR House deal with the president?"

"For any PAR lawmaker to stay in office, he would have to advance the values that he'd run on," says Jeffrey. "He'd have to stand up for what his constituents believed. So a PAR House would assert itself with the president more than the House does now."

"Are we sure that's a good thing?" asks Cassie.

"Well," says Jeffrey, "the worst presidential decisions of the last decade—waging war on Iraq, neglecting global warming, boosting the Medicare deficit—were all possible because lawmakers from both parties caved in to the president. They didn't stand up for their constituents' interests or the national interest. That's what happens when voters are asleep. But if every voter had a preferential ballot, every member of Congress would work harder for the platform that he or she had run on. Most times that would mean working out differences with the president. But sometimes, it would mean resisting the president's agenda."

"I agree," says Tom. "We need a House with more backbone. And I can see that PAR would give my colleagues stronger spines."

"Sounds right," says Cassie. "Still, we need to do more reality testing. I'm going to talk with other congressional staffers. Let's see what they think of our predictions about how a PAR House would function internally."

"Whatever questions people throw at us, I'm confident we'll come up with answers," says Tom. "If we could rattle Fran Sinclair, we should be able to hold our own with everyone else. I think we've actually figured out how Congress could resolve the issues that Washington only fights over now."

"Yes," says Jeffrey. "And to convince other folks, I'll keep track of the questions that get thrown at us and our responses. I'll put it all in a Q&A, like last time, that we can give to skeptics."*

"Fine," says Cassie. "Then what? Where do we go from here?"

"Next," says Tom, "we need a plan of action."

---

* Appendix XIII.

16

Practical First Steps

"Now that we're convinced that PAR would get lawmakers to re-solve problems they won't even address today, how do we con-vince other people—enough so they actually try PAR?" Tom asks Sidney, Cassie, and Jeffrey. They're meeting in Tom's office a week after their last session.

"We have to start on a small scale," says Cassie. "With school boards that are in trouble and town councils that are under fire."

"How do we get that ball rolling?" asks Tom. "I've been thinking about that all week. I'd like to test the waters in our district. We could invite folks to a discussion: Why American Politics Is Breaking Down—and How We Can Repair It. I'll lay out PAR and see how it flies."

"Do you think we're ready to take it out into the world?" asks Cassie.

"As ready as we'll ever be," says Tom. "We've answered the questions that people on the Hill have raised, so I should be able to answer any questions that folks back home throw at me. And the people who come to that kind of event will already be unhappy with the status quo. They'll want something better. They may respond very positively. If they don't, if regular folks don't push for PAR, it's not going to happen."

"All right," says Cassie. "I'll set up a public meeting. If the audience doesn't like what you say, I hope the word about it doesn't spread too far."

The following week, Tom flies home and drives to Greenport, a town of 12,000 just starting to recover from years of decline. He walks along the main street, where trees are starting to bloom and new shops are starting to open. Tom reaches the red brick public library that anchors a small public square. He heads to the event room in the back. About forty people have come. They vary in age from teenagers to seniors.

Tom starts the meeting by introducing himself. He says that he's dissatisfied with how Congress works and frustrated by the difficulties of representing more than 600,000 diverse residents.

Tom then asks the audience: "Would each of you tell me what you most dislike about politics today—in a sentence or so. Or tell me what you'd most like to see happen." He writes the two sets of responses on two flip charts that all can see. He promises to show the audience that what they dislike most can be fixed and that what they most want can actually materialize. He then explains how he and his staff figured out what drives most American politicians to behave so perversely and what it would take to change them. Tom senses that the audience is interested but is not yet sold on all he's telling them. He talks for only twenty minutes so he can spend most of the time answering questions.

The crowd asks probing questions, but no one is hostile. Tom feels relieved. As he answers more questions, the crowd becomes more animated.

A middle-aged man says, "What you're proposing makes sense to me. But it's also very different from what all of us are used to. How can a change this big ever happen?"

"It would have to start in school boards, town councils, and the like," says Tom. "For instance, anyone here from Johnson's Bend?"

Two people raise their hands. "What do you think of your school board?" Tom asks.

A woman who looks to be in her mid-thirties says, "It's a disaster. The board fights to a deadlock on most issues. The better-off members pull one way, the poorer members another. The empty nesters oppose the young parents. It's no wonder that our schools do an awful job of educating our kids. It's gotten so bad that our mayor keeps threatening to find some way to dissolve the board."

"What would she replace it with?" asks Tom.

"She hasn't said. You think a PAR board could solve our problem?"

"Well, each board member would be accountable to some group of townspeople. And to satisfy his or her own camp, each board member would have to negotiate with the others. The board would surely make better decisions, which most of the community might end up supporting."

"Sounds good," says the woman. "But how would we start something like that?"

"What if the mayor backed the idea?" Tom asks.

"She's popular enough that it would stir a lot of interest in town."

"I'll contact her and some other civic leaders," says Tom. "I'll plant the seeds. But it's for the people in Johnson's Bend to decide whether this is something they want to do."

The woman nods and sits down.

"Anyone here from Elmsford?" Tom asks. A well-dressed man in his fifties raises his hand. Tom continues, "I hear your planning board just issued a master plan that's been received none too well."

The man groans, "Actually, the plan has fractured my town into more camps than I ever knew existed. Every proposal has enraged some group of residents. But if you're thinking that we could elect a planning board by PAR, could the winners deal with all the technical subjects that the master plan addresses, like regional economics, land use, whatever?"

"Most planning boards hire experts to do the technical stuff. A PAR board could do the same," says Tom. "The big difference would be that on a PAR planning board, every segment of the community would have a voice in the process every step of the way. So the resulting master plan could win wide public support."

"That sounds a lot better than what's going on now," says the man. "I know plenty of folks, including two town council members, who are so angry at the planning board that they might support your idea."

"If you give me the council members' names after this meeting, I will contact them," Tom says.

A man in a tweed jacket raises his hand. "I'm wondering if we could use PAR at the state university, where I teach history. The campus is mired in controversies—over the curriculum, student drinking, and teaching assistants forming a union. The administration has met with some students and faculty members to try to figure out solutions, but every proposal so far has drawn lots of fire. So what if the faculty held a PAR election? And the students too? Those representatives and the administration might be able to thrash out solutions that all groups could accept."

"That's more likely to work than other arrangements would," says Tom.

"If I can get some of my colleagues to a meeting to discuss this idea, would you make a presentation?" asks the man. "I'm sure they'd love to go toe-to-toe with a member of Congress."

"Glad to oblige," says Tom smiling. "Let's talk after this meeting."

A middle-aged woman in jeans stands up. "The union I belong to is losing members and losing power in our dealings with companies. We're torn apart over how to deal will that. If we elected our governing council by PAR, do you think that would help?"

"If each worker felt that he or she had a real spokesperson on the governing council, wouldn't most workers feel stronger loyalty to the union?" asks Tom. "And wouldn't that make the union more effective?"

"Probably," says the woman. "But our union president would oppose giving the governing council more clout."

"Would any union members be willing to challenge your president on that score?" asks Tom.

"The head of my local is itching to run against him," says the woman. "She might like the idea. I'll run it by her if you'll give me written materials laying out the details."

"I have a two-page description of PAR that I can give you right now," says Tom. "And if you give me a week, my staff will put together a plan for how to apply it in your union. Be sure to leave me your phone number or e-mail address."

A man in a dark suit raises his hand. "I'm head of training at Scalar Electronics. Our CEO decided that we have to overhaul our product line to meet foreign competition. So he picked some employees to help him figure out a new strategy. Yet most of our workers fear that *their* concerns will be ignored. I can see how a PAR body of workers could allay that fear. But the CEO would never hand that much power to workers he hadn't personally selected."

"I understand," says Tom. "Still, you could say to your CEO: 'For a totally new strategy to work, we'd need our employees to back it to the hilt. So why not ask them to pick the people they most want to speak for them on the company's direction? You could work with that small group to develop a plan that satisfies you *and* them. Each spokesperson could then pitch the plan to the workers who'd chosen him. All the employees would feel that they'd had a say. They'd be more likely to do all they can to make the new strategy succeed.'"

"Sounds doable," says the man. "I could run the idea by the VP for Human Resources. But I'd need to give her a detailed proposal."

"My staff will work on it with you," says Tom.

After the meeting ends, Tom talks with each person to whom he's made a commitment. He leaves the library smiling.

Later, at home with Kelley, Tom tells her, "The audience started out skeptical, but they really listened to what I had to say. Most of them ended up liking the idea. I feel real hope."

The following afternoon back in Washington, sitting down again with Sidney, Cassie, and Jeffrey, Tom describes his meeting.

"You promised a lot of proposals," says Cassie. "How are you going to deliver them?"

"I planned to ask Jeffrey to draft them," says Tom. Then, turning to Jeffrey, "How would you feel about making PAR your full-time job?"

"Terrific. I've already started to design a website. It will show anyone in the country how to implement PAR in their own community. Folks can download materials to hand out to others. They can ask us questions. We can constantly update the site with new information and ideas."

"Sounds like too much for you to handle alone," says Tom.

"I'll pitch in," says Cassie. "I'll find the time. Because to figure out how to apply PAR in many kinds of local venues will require a very practical hand —mine."

"I agree," says Tom. "Jeffrey?"

"Of course," says Jeffrey. "PAR was Cassie's idea to begin with."

"One thing, though," says Cassie. "After we put in all the work, suppose some of the projects succeed. We may still never see PAR happen in the House."

"If the first people who try PAR like the results," says Tom, "neighboring communities will notice. People in other towns will insist on trying the same approach. The idea will snowball."

"And," says Jeffrey, "if PAR works well for school boards and the like, many people will demand it for their municipal elections, which they can make happen. After all, San Francisco adopted a preferential ballot years ago. And ever since, many other communities have started considering it. Local changes happen all the time."

"*How* do they happen?" asks Sidney.

"Usually by a referendum," says Jeffrey. "And in the cities that first try PAR, if most people like the results, will Americans elsewhere just watch their local governments wallow in partisan bickering? No way. Residents of other cities will agitate for the same change. PAR will spread. People will eventually apply the same pressure on their state governments."

"Maybe so," says Cassie, "but there's no such thing as a national referendum. Citizens can't force Congress to adopt PAR."

"If enough people decide that PAR is a change that we have to make, they can vote out of office any incumbents who oppose them," says Jeffrey.

"You really believe that ordinary citizens can force a change in House elections?" asks Cassie.

"It's just a matter of numbers," says Jeffrey. "Take a typical presidential election year. Usually, 50 percent of Americans don't vote, while roughly 32 percent vote for House incumbents, and 18 percent choose challengers. That means incumbents win on average by just 14 percent of the total electorate. So, what if 20 percent of Americans decide that we need a new election process? If that 20 percent, instead of not voting and instead of voting for incumbents, votes for challengers, they can remove from office nearly every incumbent who resists the change to PAR. In this way, ordinary citizens have the power to create a PAR House."

"That is a wildly ambitious—some would say radical—idea," says Cassie.

"But I'm not advocating that step now," says Jeffrey. "I just want to prove that PAR can happen—in any small town or the most powerful town in the world, this one. Even you agree that the current system is broken, that it's putting all our necks at risk, that it threatens our very survival."

"Yes. This place is a disaster waiting to happen. We have to make a change."

"And if you—after years of being attached to the current setup—can sign up for a change as big as PAR, others will too," says Jeffrey. "Fifty million Americans say they'd work to improve the political process."

"So what have they been doing all this time?" asks Cassie.

"They've been focusing their energy in the wrong direction," says Jeffrey. "Most Americans have been condemning the Republicans, the Democrats, partisanship in general, powerful interest groups, or self-serving voters—none of which are the real problem. Just about everyone in this country has been spinning their wheels. They've been stuck."

"So what's going to get them unstuck?" asks Cassie.

"Your proof that the election system is the real problem," says Sidney. "You have the facts and figures to show that every legislator has constituents too diverse to comprehend. A lawmaker today can't possibly satisfy most of his or her voters. So, instead, a typical lawmaker resorts to the bag of tricks that most of us have come to hate."

"We just need to get that case out into the world," says Jeffrey. "We need to make people understand the real reason their politicians shortchange them. Once people know what the real problem is, they'll want to fix it."

"Perhaps," says Cassie. "But PAR isn't the only solution that people will consider."

"Name any other solution that could solve all the problems we've identified," Jeffrey asks.

"I doubt that there is one."

"If PAR does all that we think it can, it'll happen."

"It's going to be a very long road," says Cassie.

"Yes, it will," says Tom. "We need to convince folks that PAR answers their biggest grievances against politicians, that it addresses their worst fears about what lies ahead, that it offers a brighter future. And we have to show folks that they can make it happen."

"I'd like to make that the main theme of our website," says Jeffrey. "And I'd like to call the site GenuineRepresentation.org."

"Good," says Tom.

Cassie stands up, crosses to the window, and looks out pensively.

"It is going to be a long road," Tom says to Cassie. "But isn't it worth the effort? Now that you've painted a picture of what *could* be, do you want to stick with what we've got?"

"No. Not any more. I can't." She then turns to Tom and says, "So let's get started."

17

A Decade From Now: Our Rejuvenated Democracy

"It's good to see you again, Congressman, after all these years," says Sidney extending his hand.

"Sidney, we go back too far for you to call me 'Congressman.'"

"Glad you feel that way, Jeffrey. How've you been?"

"Busy. There's never enough time." Jeffrey motions for Sidney to sit and does so himself. "And you?"

"Busy, too. But I'm glad you called because what you're doing here strikes me as just remarkable. How can I help?"

"Before we go into that, let's wait till Cassie arrives," says Jeffrey.

"How is she?"

"Same as always: tough as nails. And she gets things done. She's the best person to have on your side."

"You know I have a hard time imagining her as a member of Congress," says Sidney. "I can't conceive of her putting up with all the glad-handing it must require."

"She endures it," says Jeffrey smiling. "She worked so hard for so many years to make PAR happen that she *had* to participate in how it played out. And by the time she ran for a seat, she was so widely known that she drew the largest number of votes of anyone here. It cracks me up that she resisted the idea of lawmakers having different voting power and then wound up with more voting power than anyone else."

"You're not too far behind her yourself, are you?"

"Well, it's good for the ego, but you and I were right: It doesn't count all that much. Cassie and I together have less than 1 percent of the voting power in this place."

"But you have plenty of influence."

"Only because we have PAR in our blood. Whenever new situations crop up, people around here expect her and me to have the answers. Which of course we don't. The House still has its weak spots, for which Cassie and I often don't have solutions."

"Even so, you've come a long away. From my vantage point, Congress has made more progress on Social Security, the tax code, energy policy, and plenty of other issues than Capitol Hill had in the previous two decades.

"Fine. But over a decade ago, people had figured out how to make Social Security self-sustaining, how to make the tax code simpler and fairer, plus how to cut oil imports in half. We just caught up to what people outside Capitol Hill had already done."

"You've accomplished more than that," says Sidney. "Broad solutions are often easy to find. It's much harder to hammer out all the details among 435 lawmakers, win support for the whole package from the rest of the country, and then take responsibility for the results."

"Perhaps, but we still have a long way to go. Medicare will be much tougher to fix than Social Security ever was. We're not even close to consensus on what the federal role in public education should be. Plus we're still under huge pressure to do more on the tax code."

"Listen. People will never be satisfied. So for Congress to have two-thirds of the public approving of its work is some feat."

"I'm disappointed that figure isn't higher."

"Jeffrey, if I had told you when we first met that the House would someday have approval ratings approaching 70 percent, you'd have said that I was out of my mind."

"You're right. Ah, here's our number one congresswoman now." Both men stand.

"Sidney," says Cassie, striding into the room, taking off her jacket. "How the hell are you?"

"Happy to see the two of you living out your dream."

"Well, every now and then I get a rush, but most of the time this is the toughest job I've ever had. We've created enormous expectations. Now we have to live up to them."

"Would you rather be working in the House of years ago, when most Americans had dismal expectations?"

"Of course not. But it's still no picnic here."

"It'll never be a picnic. Way back when, I told you that real representatives get hit with a constant stream of tough demands."

"I remember. Now Jeffrey and I want to pick your brain about how we can come close to meeting those demands."

"Fire away," says Sidney, as they all sit.

"To start," says Cassie, "let me acknowledge that your plan for how we should organize our committees has worked out well. But we never discussed who would chair those committees, which we still haven't quite figured out. After all, each committee member is pushing an agenda for a bloc of colleagues, so no committee member will allow anyone else to control the agenda, not even the chairperson. Everyone insists that the chair be neutral. So, first we tried rotating the chair each day. But that meant some days committees would run smoothly and other days they'd be a mess. So now, to chair each committee, we appoint a lawmaker who didn't run for a seat on it and seems to have an open mind on its issues. That works better, but it's still hit or miss. Any thoughts on how to improve things?"

"You could hire professional mediators to run committee meetings," says Sidney.

"That won't fly," says Cassie. "Most members of Congress would never accept outsiders in that key a role."

"I agree," says Jeffrey.

"Okay," says Sidney. "There are plenty of ways to run meetings that will promote agreements."

"If we tried to impose new procedures here, most members would rebel," says Cassie.

"Then don't impose them. Suggest them," says Sidney. "You could organize a weekend retreat for the entire House. Even in the old days, Congress tried that a few times, although the good feelings didn't last much past the weekend. But if you organized something similar now, it would be different. Right?"

"For sure," says Cassie. "These days, nearly everyone here wants to get things done."

"So during the retreat you could discuss how to coax committees toward consensus. I can provide exercises that illustrate creative ways to put together agreements. It's stuff that I've used with corporate executives. We could tailor that to the situation here."

"They'd have to be exercises that lawmakers would actually try."

"Some CEOs I've worked with have been as tough to impress as any politician," says Sidney. "I'll put together some ideas that have intrigued even my most jaded clients. If you'll give me detailed feedback, I'm sure the three of us can come up with things that'll work."

"That's worth a shot."

"What else?" asks Sidney.

"Most House bills are drawing over 75 percent yes votes," says Cassie. "That's not bad, but many of us suspect that we can do better. Jeffrey and I remember your telling us how it helps if negotiators try to hammer out agreements on several issues at the same time. That way, they can more easily put together a package that all sides can support. We were wondering: Out of all the possible combinations of proposals, how can we find the one combination that will satisfy the most people to the greatest extent?"

"The most reliable way to do that is with computer software," says Sidney. "Each person inputs his or her preferences, and the computer comes up with the optimal combinations."

"Do you realize how controversial that would be?" asks Cassie. "I can see the headlines now: Congress Turns Its Job Over to Microsoft."

"That's not how it would work," says Sidney. "The computer doesn't write legislation. It just tests all the ways of combining the ideas that *you've* come up with. Think of it as a fancy vote-tallying machine. The beauty of it is that the computer can consider millions of combinations, which people can't possibly do. If you tried the program once and 90 percent of you ended up voting yes for the result, what would happen?"

"It'd be tough to resist," says Jeffrey. "If both an impartial computer and 90 percent of Congress backed a measure, it would have lots of legitimacy. To anyone who criticized the bill, we could say, 'Propose something better or get off our backs.'"

"I don't know," says Cassie. "Is the world ready for computerized legislation?"

"That's not a fair way to describe it," says Sidney. "People would still have to devise each proposal, assess the effects of each one, state their preferences, and then bless the final result. If they didn't approve, they could toss the results out."

"I like the idea," says Jeffrey, "because it would prove to the world how committed we are to the best possible outcomes."

"Maybe so," says Cassie, "but using computers to put together bills would give the pundits fits. The late-night talk show hosts would make jokes about it for God knows how long."

"Why don't we try this idea on a small scale?" asks Jeffrey. "If one subcommittee tried it on a very technical subject, it might not draw flak. And if all the stakeholders applauded the result, the next time we could be more ambitious."

"I could set up a meeting with a computer maven who would walk you through all the steps that would be required," says Sidney.

"I suppose there's no harm in hearing what would be involved," says Cassie.

"What else?" asks Sidney.

"What else? You must be joking," says Cassie. "We're contemplating a revolution here, and you want more?"

"Listen, PAR was the truly big revolution. The two of you did an incredible job of getting that idea out into the world."

Cassie smiles. "Don't forget Tom Hennessey," she says. "He sparked this whole effort. He started the nonprofit that promoted PAR in every state. Now, he's advocating it in other countries. He proved to be a lot tougher than most people around here gave him credit for—me included."

"How so?" asks Sidney.

"At first, I pegged him as being on the mild side. I had it all wrong. I didn't fully realize it until his last day in office. It was then that he confided in Jeffrey and me—well, confessed is more like it—that he once accosted some bully who was molesting a teenaged girl. When the guy pulled a knife on him, he beat the guy nearly to death."

"Really?"

"I had a hard time picturing Tom in that kind of brawl, too, and he looked very uncomfortable describing it. But then, he said something I'll never forget.

He said: 'I've learned that anger can be a positive force. It can rouse you to act when you have to—when you might otherwise feel too afraid.'"

"I can relate to that," says Jeffrey. "Anger at the old system kept me going many times when I was tempted to give up."

"It's good that the three of you never gave up," says Sidney. "You've made quite a difference—for many people."

"We were mostly a catalyst," says Jeffrey. "The local activists who inspired their communities to try PAR for school boards and town councils really got the ball rolling. They deserve most of the credit. They turned the tide."

"They sure did," says Cassie. "And now we have to meet the expectations of those activists and everyone else who leans on us to resolve some issue or other. So let's get to it."

Jeffrey nods at her and smiles, "Same old Cassie. Only the nuts and bolts count."

Cassie grins back at him. "Same old Jeffrey. Always in the clouds. I'm surprised you find your way to Capitol Hill every morning."

Jeffrey laughs, "It surprises most of my friends, too. All right, let's get to it."

18

Epilogue:
Back to Here and Now—What You Can Do

Will our politicians ever work for our best interests as conscientiously as this book envisions? That depends on whether people like you are willing to do your part.

If you find it hard to believe that you could make that much of a difference, we'd like to point to an event that suggests nearly all of us have more power than we admit, more power than we use. It occurred some years ago, late one night in a middle-class New York community: More than a dozen concerned citizens watched from their apartment windows as a man attacked their twenty-eight-year-old neighbor, Kitty Genovese. As the assailant stabbed Kitty repeatedly over thirty-five minutes, several neighbors shouted at him to stop. But no one took the step that could have saved Kitty's life—calling the police—until she had already bled to death. That chilling episode reminds all of us that even citizens with good intentions can be paralyzed by inertia.

That kind of inertia has infected most of us politically. For years, we all watched our leaders in Washington sabotage our nation's finances and wage a costly, destabilizing war under false pretenses. All the while, the White House and Congress left us vulnerable to the real threats: an economy overloaded with debt, an addiction to imported oil, crumbling public schools, runaway health care costs, an over-heating climate, rogue states obtaining nuclear weapons, and terrorists plotting our destruction.

How did we react? Most of us complained loudly and often about our politicians. Many of us voted for or gave money to candidates we thought could do a better job.

But after reading this book, you know that these steps cannot save us. You know that just changing the people in office cannot give us a government that does what is right, what is fair, what is in America's best interests, what is in your family's best interests.

The system itself is broken, and it's the system itself that must be fixed.

The big question is: Who will fix it? Are we waiting for someone on a white horse to come to our rescue? If so, our fate is sealed: We will be stuck with the status quo or worse.

Fortunately, if enough of us step up to the plate, *we* have the power to fix our broken government. As you saw in chapter 16 (on page 146), if 20 percent of the American people can agree on a change, that 20 percent is enough to vote out of office nearly every incumbent who tries to block our way.

So, the main obstacle to fixing the system is not (nor has it ever been) the incumbents. The obstacle to change is our own inertia.

If you want your government to work, you need to play some part. Where do you start? For openers, you can share with your friends and family any ideas in this book that appeal to you. If most readers of this book talk to people they know, then they in turn talk to their friends, and so on, we can get a large swath of the country talking about the real flaws in politics today. Once that happens, many of us will start to demand real solutions.

And if you agree that Personally Accountable Representation is the best available solution, that it would produce far better government than other election methods, you can discuss with your friends and neighbors how your own town would benefit by adopting PAR. Or you can apply PAR in your school system, in your union, or in your company. To see exactly how to start that kind of campaign, and then carry it through to completion, just visit our website: GenuineRepresentation.org

The bottom line is that you can help transform our nation's political life. You can help create a brighter future.

Are you in?

Appendixes

Appendix I
More Cases of Political Consensus

Lawmakers patted themselves on the back in the fall of 1980. The public had demanded that Washington do something to clean up the country's hazardous waste dumps, and Congress had delivered. Under the new Superfund law, any person or company that had contributed even in a small way to polluting any designated toxic site had to pay for cleaning it up. If all the parties responsible couldn't be located, then those that could be found had to foot the whole bill.

But most companies saddled with Superfund liabilities refused to pay, claiming that their role in polluting the sites had been minimal. Many firms hauled the government into court. In the decade after the Superfund law was passed, the government and private sector ended up spending three times as much money on legal bills as they did on cleanups. Business people, environmentalists, and government officials were soon lambasting the Superfund as a waste of public and private funds.

To look for a solution, the Vermont Law School's Environmental Law Center and the Keystone Center, a nonprofit that helps to resolve conflicts, jointly formed a National Commission on Superfund (NCS). They invited twenty-five environmentalists, chemical industry chief executives, and environmental officials to participate.

After meeting six times in one year, these longtime opponents hammered out a concrete proposal. They recommended that instead of the government coercing the deepest pocket to pay for cleaning up each toxic site, an administrative law judge should parcel out liability among all the parties responsible. All sides figured that administrative judges familiar with environmental law would make more informed and evenhanded decisions than juries would. The commission also proposed other improvements in the Superfund, such as having the Environmental Protection Agency assign each hazardous site a priority based on how big a risk it posed to the surrounding community.

All the commission members ended up endorsing the final report.

They then had to sell their proposal, which took some doing. For instance, when Robert Burt, head of the FMC Corporation, presented the commission's proposals to the Chemical Manufacturers Association, many CEOs balked. They demanded a deal tilted more in their companies' favor. But in private talks with CMA board members, Burt argued that the NCS proposals had a far better chance to become law than anything the industry could come up with on its own. Furthermore, the NCS proposals would save the chemical industry from the endless court battles it would continue to face if the current law remained unchanged. In time, the entire CMA board bought Burt's arguments and backed the recommendations.

Eventually, every major environmental group endorsed the proposal as well.

The commission members then approached the Clinton administration for support. They were unsuccessful, at first. Some White House staffers had their own proposal and were miffed at being left out of the NCS negotiations. Nonetheless, the commissioners eventually persuaded the West Wing that the NCS plan had the best shot to win backing in Congress. So, the administration gave its stamp of approval.

The NCS then brought its proposal to Capitol Hill. Unfortunately, the 1994 elections were approaching, which meant that Republicans leaders wanted to deny the Democratic White House any legislative victories. So the Republicans blocked the NCS measure. Instead, they promised industry chieftains a more favorable deal once the GOP won control of Congress.

But even now, more than a decade later, that better deal still has not materialized.

To be fair, in this story and others like it in chapter 1, a small group of adversaries met in private, sheltered from public view. Legislators, however, work in the constant glare of media attention. Might that difference be a major reason that lawmakers do a poorer job?

The facts say otherwise. Plenty of adversaries have attracted publicity, yet still have done better work than lawmakers.

In 1997, for example, attorneys general (AGs) from forty states drew front-page headlines when they sued the major tobacco companies. The AGs intended to recover the money that their states had spent to treat tobacco-related illnesses. The company CEOs responded by offering to negotiate with the attorneys general and the most vocal antismoking groups. After four months, the negotiators hammered out a deal that would have settled all lawsuits against the companies and created programs to curb teenage smoking. While all the parties admitted that the pact had flaws, they also insisted that everyone would do better with the deal than under the status quo.

There was one problem, though. For the agreement to take effect, Congress had to enact it. Yet as soon as lawmakers began to debate, the deal began to unravel. Some legislators insisted that the tobacco companies had harmed so many people that they should pay far more money than they'd agreed to, which the firms refused to consider. Meanwhile, other lawmakers—most of whom had received large contributions from the tobacco industry—argued that the companies would pass the costs of any settlement on to smokers, most of whom were poor. So the higher the settlement, the more the poor would pay. On that pretext, those lawmakers blocked a higher settlement. Each faction refused to budge until Congress deadlocked over the issue. As a result, the deal died.

After licking their wounds, the attorneys general and the tobacco company lawyers started negotiating again. Eventually, they settled their lawsuits. But to ensure that their agreement didn't require congressional approval, the negotiators had to drop most of the provisions to curb teenage smoking.

So, who benefited from Congress's stalemate? Certainly not the public.

At the local level, there are thousands of such stories. One made front-page news in New York City because it concerned risks to the city's water supply, one of the purest in the country. At the time, the early 1990s, towns around the city's rural reservoirs were producing increasing amounts of waste products that polluted the city's water. The city reacted by using its right of eminent domain to seize the land that generated the most pollutants. The towns protested that the seized land could no longer be used for farming or any other business that paid local taxes, which was bound to hobble the towns economically.

To complicate matters, the Environmental Protection Agency entered the fray. The EPA declared that despite the city's land seizures, its water supply was growing contaminated enough that it would eventually fall below federal standards. The EPA ordered the city to build filtration plants that would cost $5 billion. Unable to afford that kind of money, the city seized even more rural land and threatened to arrest those who polluted its reservoirs.

Officials from the affected towns blasted New York City in the media. City officials reciprocated.

People on all sides felt beleaguered enough that when the governor of New York State invited the key players to meet in early 1996, all sides accepted.

In time, officials from the state, the city, the rural towns, the EPA, and several environmental groups negotiated a pact: The towns would take steps to cut pollution so that the city's water supply would meet EPA standards. In return, the city would curb its use of eminent domain, start buying land around its reservoirs on the open market, and pay taxes on that land to the local communities.

While some citizens on each side opposed making any concessions to the other parties, most people accepted the deal's logic. Fortunately, the deal took effect without needing approval from the New York State legislature, which most analysts consider even more dysfunctional than Congress.

Some legislatures have even admitted that the parties directly involved in a dispute can negotiate a better solution than lawmakers can. For instance, in 1995 Oregon's state legislature mandated that battles over land use be resolved by the groups most directly involved.

That measure was the result of a dispute the year before. The state's Department of Transportation had wanted to make Oregon's rural roads safer without meeting all the environmental requirements for that kind of work. The state's Department of Land Conservation protested that keeping the countryside pristine mattered as much as drivers' safety. When the two departments asked the state legislature to resolve the matter, most lawmakers wanted no part of that dispute. They insisted that the two departments work it out.

Unable to make progress on their own, the two agencies approached groups with the largest stake in the issue, including farmers, environmentalists, businesses, county engineers, and the state's planning directors. Each group picked a spokesperson. After meeting five times, the representatives hammered out a proposal that all of them supported. The heads of both agencies gladly accepted the plan, as did the state legislature.

Oregon lawmakers liked the result so much that they passed a bill directing that other battles over land use be resolved in the same way: by assembling a task force of stakeholders.

But that ending was an exception. Most lawmakers won't cede authority, even to groups that can solve problems that those lawmakers cannot or will not.

Appendix II
How the Major Issues Have Shifted Over Time

America began as an agrarian society. At its start, the major issues were slavery, tariffs, and westward expansion. All of these subjects hinged on geography.

But after the Civil War, America began to emerge as an industrial giant. As a result, the poor, the middle class, and the rich began to collide more often. Starting in the late nineteenth century, Congress responded to the changing conditions by:

- Creating the Interstate Commerce Commission to stop railroads from price gouging
- Passing the Sherman Antitrust Act to break up monopolies controlling many industries
- Passing the Pure Food and Drug Act to regulate the quality of food and drugs
- Forming the Federal Reserve System to regulate banks and interest rates
- Creating the Federal Trade Commission to control false advertising and price collusion
- Passing the Clayton Antitrust Act to punish firms that stifled competition

In these issues, geography's role was minimal. Instead, each citizen's concerns depended on his or her economic situation and political values.

This trend accelerated when the Great Depression of the 1930s left 25 percent of Americans out of work. More than ever, politics revolved around the question of how much government should protect citizens from economic adversity. Prodded by President Franklin Roosevelt, Congress intervened in the economy on an unprecedented scale by:

- Creating the Securities and Exchange Commission to regulate the financial markets
- Establishing the Federal Deposit Insurance Corporation to insure depositors' savings

- Passing the Social Security Act to fund workers' retirements
- Creating the National Labor Relations Board to protect workers' rights to form unions
- Passing the Fair Labor Standards Act to set a minimum wage for the first time

Where citizens stood on these issues depended on their finances, family situations, or political values—far more than on their location. The same has held true for most major issues since Roosevelt's time, including:

- The creation of Medicare and Medicaid to guarantee health care to the poor and elderly
- President Lyndon Johnson's War on Poverty
- The civil rights legislation of the mid-1960s
- The Vietnam War
- The major environmental legislation of the 1970s
- President Ronald Reagan's tax cuts
- President Bill Clinton's efforts to make health care universally available
- President George W. Bush's tax cuts
- The 2003 war in Iraq

In 2008, most people cite as their top concerns: the economy, national security, health care, Social Security, and taxes. On these issues, where a person lives is largely irrelevant. What counts are each person's income, age, household type, and political values.

APPENDIX III
How America Became More Diverse Over Time

The charts on the following pages show the percentage of Americans in different categories from 1790 to 2000. The charts indicate that the American people have become far more diverse over time. Therefore, it has become much harder for Congress to represent us.

The first chart shows the percentage of adults in each of six job categories:

- farmers
- laborers, operators, and service workers
- craftsmen
- administrative support workers
- professionals and managers
- non-labor force over sixty-five

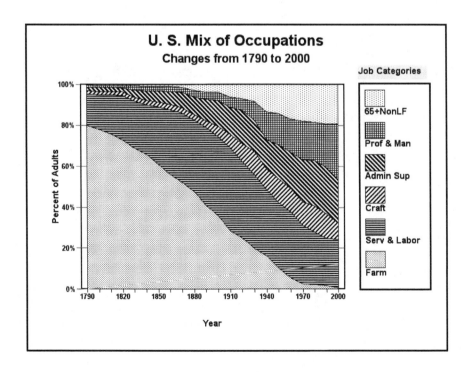

(Note: The census first collected job data in 1870, so this chart extrapolates the 1870 data back to 1790.)

This chart shows America shifting from 80 percent farmers to large numbers of us filling the five other categories. Each heading also includes about a hundred subcategories that didn't exist in the eighteenth century. Laborers, for instance, used to work mostly for local farmers. Now, laborers cover a much wider range that includes making toys, operating cranes, and building jumbo jets. Professionals and managers used to be mostly country lawyers and doctors. Now, they too cover a much wider gamut, from purchasing agents to psychologists and aeronautical engineers.

AMERICANS BECOME MORE DIVERSE BY INCOME

To compare how economically diverse Americans are today versus how diverse we were two centuries ago, we need to look at the census of home values conducted in 1798 because the U.S. Census didn't collect income data until the mid-twentieth century. Then, to compare income distribution now and in 1798, let's assume that the value of a person's home (whether owned or rented) roughly correlated with his or her income.

Next, we need to segment the data from each time period into the same number of brackets. So, the chart below has ten equal brackets plus an eleventh that includes everyone above the tenth.

For 1798, the chart shows the percent of homes in each $50 bracket.

For 2000, the chart shows the percent of incomes in each $10,000 bracket.

Comparing Distribution of Home Values in 1798 to Distribution of Incomes in 2000			
HOME VALUES IN 1798	**% OF HOMES IN 1798**	**% OF INCOMES IN 2000**	**INCOMES IN 2000**
$0–50	38.9	9.9	$0–10K
$50–100	12.1	12.7	$10–20K
$100–150	11.0	13.0	$20–30K
$150–200	**7.3**	**12.2**	$30–40K
$200–250	**4.3**	**10.6**	$40–50K
$250–300	**3.7**	**9.0**	$50–60K
$300–350	**3.2**	**7.5**	$60–70K
$350–400	**2.7**	**5.6**	$70–80K
$400–450	**2.1**	**4.2**	$80–90K
$450–500	**1.8**	**3.1**	$90–100K
$500+	12.9	12.2	$100K+

This chart indicates that 60 percent of early Americans were concentrated in the lowest three income brackets. The middle brackets made up a quarter of the population, while 13 percent reached the top rung.

Industrialization then spread the wealth. The middle class—from $30,000 to $100,000— has doubled to comprise half of us. Each of the middle brackets (data in bold) has in fact roughly doubled as a percentage of the population.

AMERICANS BECOME MORE DIVERSE BY AGE

The chart below indicates how age groups that barely existed in early America —the middle aged and the elderly—have exploded in numbers.

(Note: The first census only counted two age categories, under sixteen and over sixteen. So, in this chart, age data from the mid-1800s has been extrapolated back to 1790.)

In 1790, about 60 percent of the population was younger than twenty-one. Most Americans then, if living today, wouldn't be old enough to order a beer. The vast majority of adults were between the ages of twenty-one and forty-four. Those we now consider middle-aged, forty-five to sixty-four year olds, were less than 9 percent of the total. Seniors were inconsequential in number.

By the year 2000, the percentage of forty-five to sixty-four year olds had more than doubled to about 22 percent. The percentage of seniors had quintupled.

In short, where once only two age groups dominated, today at least four age groups have politically significant numbers.

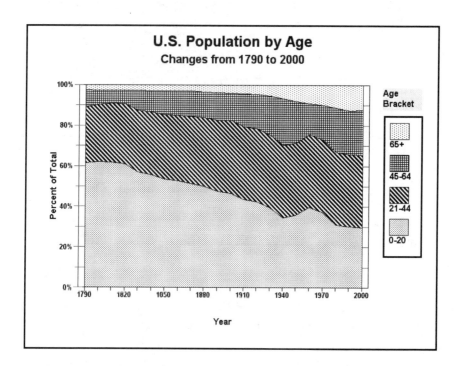

HOUSEHOLDS BECOME MORE DIVERSE

The chart below indicates how, over time, U.S. households have become smaller and more varied.

Most early Americans lived in families with seven or more people. Couples without children were just 5 percent of the population. The number of singles was tiny.

By the year 2000, singles comprised 9 percent of the public. Two-person households had become the largest category. And households between three and five members all expanded as a proportion of the population.

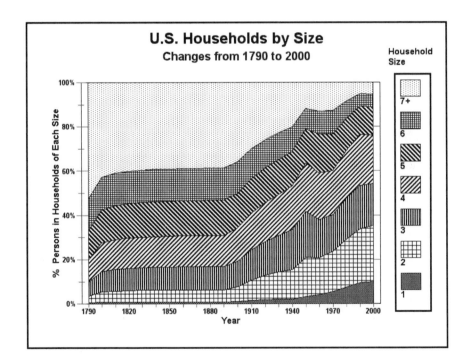

Appendix IV
James Madison's Views on Representation

On the Need for Voters to Hold Lawmakers Accountable
(from The Federalist, *Nos. 51, 52, and 57)*

"If angels were to govern men, neither external nor internal controuls on government would be necessary.... A dependence on the people is no doubt the primary controul on the government."

"[I]t is particularly essential that the [House of Representatives] should have an immediate dependence on, and an intimate sympathy with, the people. Frequent elections are unquestionably the only policy by which this dependence and sympathy can be effectually secured."

"The aim of every political constitution is, or ought to be, first to obtain for rulers men who possess most wisdom to discern, and most virtue to pursue, the common good of the society; and in the next place, to take the most effectual precautions for keeping them virtuous."

"[T]he House of Representatives is so constituted as to support in the members an habitual recollection of their dependence on the people.... [Representatives] will be compelled to anticipate the moment when ... their exercise of [power] is to be reviewed, and when they must [surrender power] unless a faithful discharge of their trust shall have established their title to a renewal of it."

"Duty, gratitude, interest, ambition itself are the chords by which [Representatives] will be bound to fidelity and sympathy with the great mass of the people. ... are [these connections] not all that ... human prudence can devise?"

On Aligning Each Representative With His Constituents' Interests
(from The Federalist, *No. 56)*

"It is a sound and important principle that the representative ought to be acquainted with the interests and circumstances of his constituents.

[Referring to his own times:] "Divide the largest State into ten or twelve districts, and . . . there will be no peculiar local interests . . . which will not be within the knowledge of the representative of the district."

[Again, about his own times:] "Taking each State by itself, its laws are the same, and its interests but little diversified. . . . At present some of the States are little more than a society of husbandmen."

"[I]ndustry [will] give a variety and complexity to the affairs of a nation. [Industry] will . . . be the fruits of a more advanced population; and will require . . . fuller representation."

On How Congress Would Serve the National Interest
(from The Federalist, *No.10)*

"The effect of [government by a small number of citizens elected by the rest is] to refine and enlarge the public views."

"By enlarging too much the number of [voters], you render the representative too little acquainted with all their local circumstances and lesser interests; as by reducing [the number of voters] too much, you render [the representative] unduly attached to these [local interests], and too little fit to comprehend and pursue great and national objects. The Federal Constitution forms a happy combination in this respect."

"[T]ake in a greater variety of parties and interests; and you make it less probable that a majority . . . will have a common motive to invade the rights of other citizens; or [be able] to act in unison [on such a motive]."

APPENDIX V
Demographics in 98 Percent of Congressional Districts

Percent of People in Each Age Bracket		
AGE BRACKET	**PERCENT OF U.S. POPULATION**	**PERCENT OF POPULATION IN 98% OF CONGRESSIONAL DISTRICTS**
0–14	21%	14–28%
15–24	14%	10–19%
25–44	30%	25–37%
45–64	22%	17–27%
65 and over	12%	5–19%

Percent of Households in Each Family Category		
HOUSEHOLD TYPE	**PERCENT OF U.S. POPULATION**	**PERCENT OF POPULATION IN 98% OF CONGRESSIONAL DISTRICTS**
Married with children	24%	12–35%
Married without children	28%	16–35%
Nontraditional Family (mostly single parents)	16%	10–31%
Nonfamily (mostly singles)	32%	18–46%

Percent of Workers in Each Job Category		
JOB CATEGORY	**PERCENT OF U.S. POPULATION**	**PERCENT OF POPULATION IN 98% OF CONGRESSIONAL DISTRICTS**
Professional/Manager	34%	18–50%
Administrative Support	27%	22–31%
Craftsmen	9%	5–15%
Service & Labor	30%	17–43%
Farmers	1%	0–3%

APPENDIX VI
Why Politicians Pass Up the Best Energy Policy

Why have American politicians let our country become addicted to foreign oil, thereby endangering our security, our economy, and our environment? To uncover the main reason, consider one energy policy that would benefit nearly every American: substantially raising the taxes on gasoline and other carbon-based fuels, while cutting income taxes an equivalent amount.

Here's how this plan would work: Suppose gasoline taxes were raised by $1.50 a gallon. To save some of that money, most Americans would buy more fuel-efficient cars. Others would drive fewer miles. Many of us would do both.

The higher gas tax would of course be a burden on a typical family, costing about $1,000 a year. But the government could neutralize that burden by giving *every* family a credit of $1,000 on their Social Security or income taxes. Financially, the typical American would come out even. Citizens who cut their gas consumption the most would do even better. They'd end up with extra cash in their pockets.

Now compare this plan to what Congress did in late 2007: It required car companies to increase the fuel efficiency of their products by 30 percent over a period of thirteen years. By contrast, a big hike in the gas tax would motivate nearly every adult and every business to look for the most convenient and cost-effective ways to cut their own gas consumption. The whole country would work on the problem, not just a few car companies.

In fact, if carbon-based fuels were taxed heavily, venture capitalists and entrepreneurs would invest far more than they do now in looking for cost-effective alternatives. And entrepreneurs are more likely to find practical alternatives faster and more cheaply than if politicians or government bureaucrats decide what alternative energy sources to invest in.

Carbon taxes would also work better than the cap-and-trade system that Europe uses to limit carbon dioxide emissions. With cap-and-trade, the government allocates each business an exact amount of carbon dioxide that it's permitted to produce. Every industry lobbies for a higher quota, with no clearly fair way to decide each one's quota. The process is highly political. By contrast, with a carbon tax, including one on gasoline, everyone producing carbon dioxide could be taxed at the same rate, which would be fair to all.

So, who would oppose this plan? Given conservatives' opposition to higher taxes, would they object? In fact, most conservatives object to income taxes more than to any other kind. And a higher gas levy would let us *lower* income taxes. Plus if America used substantially less gas, we would be far less beholden to Middle East dictatorships that control most of the world's oil reserves. Billions of dollars a year that we now send to our potential enemies abroad would stay right here. Most conservatives would love that outcome.

Wouldn't car companies fight against a higher gas tax? In fact, the major car companies and other business associations have advocated a hike in gas taxes—because most CEOs know that we have to reduce our dependence on foreign oil and slow down global warming. At the same time, most corporate executives hate when the government forces their companies to take specific actions. That's one big advantage of higher gas taxes: they wouldn't force anyone to do a thing. Consumers would still decide what to buy. Businesses would still decide what to produce.

How would typical voters react to this plan? In a New York Times/CBS News poll, 85 percent of adults opposed a higher gas tax. However, when told that the effects would be less gasoline consumption and less global warming, 59 percent of Americans said they were in favor. In other words, when the benefits are explained to them, most voters support higher gas taxes.

So, why isn't it happening? Because every politician knows that most voters wouldn't listen to *them* make the case for higher gas taxes. Most voters have contempt for their politicians. So most politicians don't dare make a case for hard decisions that they know to be right.

The bottom line is that if we want Congress to enact a wise energy policy, we will have to give voters a solid reason to believe in their politicians.

APPENDIX VII
Evaluating Proportional Representation

Proportional representation (PR) has at least one clear advantage over America's system of one-winner-per-district elections: With PR, nearly every voter knows that his or her political values will be represented. Therefore, citizens have a greater incentive to become informed and to vote.

Even so, all but one of the twenty-two U.S. cities that tried PR voted to rescind it. So PR also has major disadvantages over America's current system

To understand PR's pros and cons, we need to look at the various kinds. There are two basic types: candidate based and party based.

In party-based PR, each party submits a slate of candidates to voters. On Election Day, each voter chooses one party's slate. Each party then gets seats in the legislature in rough proportion to the total number of votes it won. If the Christian Democratic Party in Holland gets 30 percent of the votes, for instance, it gets 30 percent of the parliamentary seats.

Each country also sets a minimum percentage of votes that a party must receive to get any seats. In most countries, this threshold is 5 percent. In some, it's as low as 1 percent.

In addition, a country has to decide whether each party will submit one list for the whole nation or a separate list for each region.

There are several variations on this process. In a closed list system, the leaders of each party choose its candidates and their order on the list. Those highest on the list fill the party's seats. In other words, if a party wins twenty seats, the first twenty candidates on the list fill them.

In an open list system, each voter picks a party and can also pick a particular candidate on that party's list. A candidate who receives enough votes moves higher on the list. Typically, though, most voters just designate a party and forgo their right to choose a candidate. So party leaders' initial rankings usually prevail.

A third variation on this concept is called unordered party lists. This method, which has much in common with candidate-based systems, is used in Finland. The country is divided into fifteen districts, with an average of thirteen legislators in each. In a typical district, as many as thirty candidates compete. On Election Day, each voter chooses one candidate. However, the seats go to each *party* in rough proportion to the number of votes that *all* of its candidates in the district received. The parties drawing the most votes get a slight edge. For instance, if the most popular party in a district gets 35 percent of the votes, that party gets 45 percent of the district's seats. (The exact formula? You don't want to know.) Each party's first seat goes to its most popular candidate, its second seat goes to its second most popular candidate, and so on.

Party lists can be combined with single-member districts in what's called a mixed member system. On Election Day, each citizen receives two ballots. On one ballot, he or she can vote for one of several candidates competing to represent that district. On a separate ballot, each citizen can vote for one political party. The winner of each district election gets a seat in Parliament. The rest of the seats go to the political parties.

The party list seats can be allocated in one of two ways. In a mixed member proportional (MMP) system, each party's *total* number of seats is proportional to the number of votes it received in the party list voting. Suppose, for instance, a parliament has a hundred seats, fifty of which come from the districts. Say the Social Democrats win fifteen district seats, and 40 percent of the party list vote. The Social Democrats would then get twenty-five party list seats on top of their fifteen district seats, thereby giving them 40 percent of all one-hundred seats. Germany, Italy, Mexico, and New Zealand use MMP.

In a parallel system, the party list seats are allocated separately from the district seats. So, if the Unity Party wins 20 percent of the party list vote, it gets 20 percent of the party list seats no matter how many district seats it won. Japan, South Korea, and Thailand use a parallel system.

Then, there are the candidate-based versions of proportional representation. Typically, a country is divided into districts, with each district having at least three representatives. Ten or more candidates may run for those seats.

There are three basic variations on this arrangement. With cumulative voting (CV), each voter gets as many votes as there are seats to fill in that district, and he or she can allocate those votes to several candidates or to just one of them. This feature helps minorities wins seats. That is, minority voters can allot all their votes to one candidate, thereby magnifying his or her odds of winning. The Illinois House of Representatives used CV from 1870 to 1980.

Another candidate-based system is the single nontransferable vote

(SNTV). On Election Day, each voter chooses one candidate. The candidates drawing the most votes in each district win its seats. Afghanistan uses SNTV.

The third type of candidate-based PR is the single transferable vote (STV). It's the system that twenty-two American cities tried in the first half of the twentieth century. Ireland still uses it. On Election Day, each voter receives a preferential ballot on which he or she is asked to rank the candidates from his first choice to his last. The winners in each district are chosen by a complex formula designed to give as many voters as is practical at least one representative they can accept.

How do these systems stack up against America's one-winner-per-district elections? To answer that question precisely, we'd have to analyze each PR country's politics in detail. Some political scientists have tried to do just that, such as Harvard's Pippa Norris in *Election Engineering*. However, most Americans would not even consider switching to another country's system unless they were convinced that that country's political process was clearly superior to America's. No scholar we know of has shown that any country can meet that standard. So analyzing each country in detail would be of little practical value to us. The following analysis of PR will therefore stick to generalizations.

Let's first consider STV, which twenty-two American cities tried and twenty-one repealed. Why did that happen? The answer depends on whom you ask.

PR advocates claim that many voters objected to minorities winning more representation than they had in the past. In addition, the Republican and Democratic parties lost their legislative monopoly, so they fought STV vigorously. Plus, before computers, it took weeks to count STV ballots and determine who won. PR advocates say that irritated many voters.

But these explanations don't explain much. After all, if most people living under STV believed that it had improved the quality of their city government, would they have rescinded it? Not likely. If STV had improved city life, most voters would have stuck with it even if they disliked waiting for the election results, even if they disliked having minorities on the city council, and even if the two major parties objected.

In fact, many voters living under STV felt that it had *reduced* the quality of their city government. Various political scientists have acknowledged as much in a landmark book about STV's history in the United States, *Proportional Representation and Electoral Reform in Ohio*, edited by PR advocate Kathleen Barber. Cleveland voters, for instance, were disillusioned by PR's "failures to prevent partisan deals, patronage, bribery, and graft."

So, what aspects of STV might have led voters to conclude that it was responsible for poor governance?

For one thing, with STV, a typical voter does not have a specific person as his or her representative. Meanwhile, no lawmaker has a bloc of constituents who are exclusively his or her responsibility. No lawmaker even knows who his or her constituents are. How then can a lawmaker explain his actions to his voters? He has to rely on the media. But the media don't give politicians unlimited space or airtime to justify their policy decisions in detail to their supporters. How then can a lawmaker draw voters' attention enough to win reelection? The most efficient strategies are to publicly attack ideological opponents, to get pork for the district, and to assist citizens in dealing with the local bureaucracy. In other words, STV rewards lawmakers for similar tactics as their counterparts use in a one-winner-per-district system.*

Does party list PR work any better? What most distinguishes party lists from candidate-based PR is that party leaders wield a great deal of power. After all, party leaders decide each lawmaker's rank on the party list, which determines each lawmaker's odds of winning and keeping a seat. So, most rank-and-file lawmakers cater to party leaders far more than to voters.

What are party leaders after? Power, most of all. And if any party obtains a majority of seats in Parliament, it controls the legislative agenda. In most PR countries, though, no one party gets a majority of the seats. Instead, the party with the most seats usually forms a coalition with other parties. Thus, a typical party leader's top goal is to come as close as possible to winning a majority, or at least become part of the majority coalition. Meanwhile, parties outside the majority coalition constantly try to break up the ruling clique.

In this jockeying for power, party leaders often try to gain the upper hand by drawing media attention. Each party tries to show voters that it's championing its voters' interests. One popular strategy is to attack ideological opponents.

---

* More about STV is in Appendix XI.

While this combativeness may help some parties turn their legislative agendas into law in the short term, it has the opposite effect in the long term. After all, at each election, a new majority coalition can come into power and undo the policies of the previous government.

If party leaders genuinely wanted their legislative agendas to endure over time, the most reliable strategy would be to reach "grand bargains" with other parties, bargains that would last whichever party had the upper hand. While that does happen, it's rare. Why?

Because nearly all party leaders are after power today or as soon thereafter as possible. And lawmakers in each party tend to do what their party leaders want—because lawmakers in each party are beholden to party leaders far more than to voters.

These are, of course, broad generalizations. But the bottom line remains that the current forms of PR are not designed to promote constructive agreements among opposing political camps.

APPENDIX VIII
A Case for Two-Member Districts

To Americans who favor a two-party system, preferential elections in two-member districts would have clear advantages over the current election method. To begin with, in most districts, one representative would come from the right of center, the other from the left—one Republican and one Democrat. So most voters would get a representative on their half of the political spectrum. Most voters would therefore care what their representative did more than they care now. Voters would thus keep closer track of what legislators did than now.

What's more, at election time, each incumbent would compete mostly against candidates from his or her *own* part of the spectrum. So, most incumbents would have little reason to bash the opposing party. And if lawmakers bickered less, they'd accomplish far more than they do now.

Still, in some districts, both winners would come from the same party, but only if voters favored that party over the other by more than two to one. Here's why: Suppose that 65 percent of a district leaned to the right of center while 35 percent leaned left. In a preferential election, the votes of most citizens on the left would likely end up going to the district's most popular Democrat, while the votes of most citizens on the right would likely be spilt among the district's two most popular Republicans. That means one of those two would have less than 33 percent of the total votes, while the Democrat would have 35 percent. So, the Democrat would win one seat, while the most popular Republican would win the other.

Which, though, is better: two- or three-member districts? As with everything in politics, people will disagree. Three-member districts have at least one clear advantage: citizens in all three main camps—conservatives, liberals, and centrists—could be represented.

Appendix IX

The Size of Districts Proposed for Each State

The table below shows how to minimize the number of districts with less than three representatives, and then minimize the number of districts with more than three representatives.

Districts Proposed for Each State					
State's Number of House Seats	States	Proposed Number of Districts with:			
		One Rep	Two Reps	Three Reps	Four Reps
1	Alaska, Delaware, Montana, North Dakota, South Dakota, Vermont, Wyoming	1			
2	Hawaii, Idaho, Maine, New Hampshire, Rhode Island		1		
3	Nebraska, Nevada, New Mexico, Utah, West Virginia			1	
4	Arkansas, Kansas, Mississippi				1
5	Connecticut, Iowa, Oklahoma, Oregon		1	1	
6	Kentucky, South Carolina			2	
7	Alabama, Colorado, Louisiana			1	1
8	Arizona, Maryland, Minnesota, Wisconsin				2
9	Indiana, Missouri, Tennessee, Washington			3	
10	Massachusetts			2	1
11	Virginia			1	2
13	Georgia, New Jersey, North Carolina			3	1
15	Michigan			5	
18	Ohio			6	

STATE'S NUMBER OF HOUSE SEATS	STATES	PROPOSED NUMBER OF DISTRICTS WITH:			
		ONE REP	TWO REPS	THREE REPS	FOUR REPS
19	Illinois, Pennsylvania			5	1
25	Florida			7	1
29	New York			7	2
32	Texas			8	2
53	California			15	2
	Total Number of Districts with:	One Rep	Two Reps	Three Reps	Four Reps
		7	9	98	29

How Personally Accountable Representation
Would Affect Drawing of Districts

When state legislatures draw districts, they have to abide by the principle of one person, one vote. Today, with each district having one lawmaker, that means each district has to have roughly equal population.

With PAR, though, state legislatures would have more flexibility. For instance, take a typical state with six million residents and nine House seats. One option would be to draw three three-member districts with two million residents in each. Each lawmaker would then get voting power in proportion to the number of his voters. A lawmaker who drew 30 percent of the district's votes would get 30 percent of its three votes in the House, or .9 votes

Alternatively, the state legislature could draw three districts with slightly different populations. One reason for doing this would be so that each district could conform to more natural boundaries. In that case, however, each district would have to get voting power in proportion to its population. So if one district had 2.2 million residents, 10 percent more than the average, it would have to get 10 percent more voting power, or a total of 3.3 votes in the House. And again, each lawmaker would get a share of that voting power in proportion to the number of his or her voters.

Admittedly, this adds some complexity to PAR. But a House that can actually solve America's problems should be worth some complexity.

PAR would also dramatically reduce the effects of gerrymandering. To see how, we need to look at why legislators gerrymander districts. Typically, it's to achieve one of more of the following goals: (1) to help their own party win more seats than it would if districts were drawn objectively; (2) to help incumbents get reelected; or (3) to prevent minorities from obtaining seats. Let's consider these goals one at a time.

First, to help their party win more seats, legislators often concentrate voters for other parties into a few districts. In 2003, for instance, the Texas legislature redrew the state's congressional districts so that Republicans would win more congressional seats in 2004 than they had in 2002. The legislature accomplished that shift by concentrating Democratic voters into fewer districts. As a result, six more districts were left with Republican majorities.

However, if each district had three representatives and each of them was given voting power in proportion to the size of his or her constituency, concentrating voters from one party into fewer districts would just give them more power in those districts and less power in others. Still, the legislature could draw districts to scatter smaller groups so thinly that they would elect fewer than their fair share of representatives. For instance, suppose a state's voters consisted of 40 percent liberals, 40 percent conservatives, and 20 percent centrists. Legislators could draw most districts to include so few centrists that they would be unable to elect anyone in those districts. Centrists would thus end up with fewer than their fair share of seats. However, the centrists could wield power by casting their preferential votes for candidates they favored from other parties.

Second, to help incumbents get reelected, legislators often draw each district's boundaries to increase the number of voters from the incumbent's party. However, if voters had preferential ballots and an incumbent did a poor job, even voters from his or her own party would be less likely to pick him as their first choice. In other words, if voters had preferential ballots, drawing district boundaries to add more voters from an incumbent's party would constitute far less of a gift than it does now.

Third, to disempower a specific minority, legislators often draw district boundaries to split up that minority among several districts. The minority then has too few voters in any district to elect the winner. However, if each district had three legislators and each of them has power proportional to his or her constituency, preventing a sizable group from electing anyone would be much tougher to do than it is today. In addition, a preferential ballot would help minorities aggregate their votes. For instance, if most blacks in a district voted for blacks for all of their top choices, the votes of most blacks would end up going to the most popular black candidate. The black community would thus have better odds of electing someone.

The bottom line is that PAR's three features—preferential ballots, multimember districts, and proportional voting power—would make gerrymandering much less of a problem than it is today.

Single Transferable Vote Versus Personally Accountable Representation

The single transferable vote, STV, is the proportional system that twenty-two U.S. cities tried between 1915 and the 1950s. Cambridge, Massachusetts, still uses STV. So does Ireland. First designed by Thomas Hare of Great Britain in the 1850s, STV has been modified many times since.

STV relies on a preferential ballot. Voters rank the candidates they prefer, in order. However, Hare rejected the idea of some legislators having more voting power than others. To avoid that inequality, in an STV election, votes for the *most* popular candidates are transferred to *less* popular candidates.

To see how this works in practice, let's take a concrete example. Suppose a district is electing three representatives, and 1.2 million citizens turn out to vote. Under STV, the number of votes needed to win a seat is:

1 + (Number of votes cast) / (Number of seats to be filled + 1)

In this case, to win would take 1 + 1,200,000/(3+1) = 300,001 votes.

So, if the most popular candidate draws 500,001 votes, 200,000 of those are considered "excess." Those excess votes then go to his or her voters' second choices. To decide which of the 500,001 votes are excess, ballots used to be picked at random.

Nowadays, however, a fraction of each vote for the most popular candidate goes to other candidates. So in the above example, each voter for the most popular candidate would have 40 percent of his or her vote go to his or her second choice. Then, if any candidate reaches 300,001 votes, he or she is also declared a winner and the excess votes are transferred to other candidates.

What if no candidate draws 300,001 votes? Then the lowest-drawing candidates are eliminated one by one, and their votes are transferred to the next candidates on those ballots. Eventually, three candidates will end up with more than 300,001 votes.

Unsurprisingly, STV strikes many people as tough to understand, and even arbitrary.

An even bigger drawback is that STV undercuts the link between each representative and his or her constituents. For instance, in the example above, 500,001 people who want to be represented by person A are *required* to give 40 percent of their votes—in effect 40 percent of their clout—to other representatives. So while STV uses a preferential ballot, it does not adhere to voters' preferences.

Just as troubling, each STV lawmaker must share constituents with other lawmakers. Who, then, represents each voter? With STV, it's ambiguous, at best.

Furthermore, representatives who share constituents will almost always have different agendas. For instance, the excess votes of the most ardent liberal in the race will necessarily end up going to lawmakers closer to the center. How, then, can those centrist legislators explain to their liberal voters that their actions serve those voters' priorities? Their actions don't.

Communities that use STV could ask voters to identify themselves to their representative by mailing him or her a card, as they would with personally accountable representation (PAR). Most citizens would of course send the card to the person they wanted to be their representative, not their lower choices. So those lawmakers who won seats because of votes transferred from more popular candidates would *not* be accountable to many of the voters who had put them in office. Would that arrangement work? Sounds far-fetched.

In short, with STV, it's unclear whom each lawmaker represents, unclear who each lawmaker is accountable to. It's not surprising that most Americans exposed to STV have rejected it.

To be fair, STV works reasonably well in Ireland. However, Ireland is a parliamentary country.* That means the majority in Parliament picks the prime minister (PM), who picks the cabinet and more or less sets national policy. For all practical purposes, Parliament does not craft policy. It can ratify or reject the PM's decisions. It can even sack him or her with a simple majority vote. But it has much less of a role in shaping policy than an American legislature. So the situations are not comparable.

The bottom line is that if a country simply wants to decide which party should get the bulk of power, then STV is a reasonable way to count ballots. But STV is not a well-constructed system of representation.

---

* Appendix XIV.

Appendix XII
How Preferential Ballots Can Improve Any Election

If we used preferential ballots for all elections—including for mayors, governors, and the president—nearly every voter would feel positively about their choice of candidates. And the winning candidate would be guaranteed to have support from a majority of voters.

For instance, imagine if the 2008 presidential election had worked this way: In the spring, each major party held one nationwide primary that picked *several* candidates to run in the general election. Other candidates got on the ballot by gathering a million signatures on petitions.

On Election Day, our choices might have included the following:

John McCain
Barack Obama
Hillary Clinton
Mike Huckabee
John Edwards
Mitt Romney
Mike Bloomberg
Rudy Giuliani
Ron Paul
Dennis Kucinich
Bob Barr
Ralph Nader

Now suppose that on Election Day each of us received a preferential ballot. In that case, anyone who backed *any* of these candidates would have a good reason to vote. Even if your favorite candidate couldn't win, you could pick him or her as your first choice and more popular candidates as lower choices. You could vote your conscience, without wasting your vote.

In addition, if every voter had a preferential ballot, a candidate could win only by appealing to a broad spectrum of voters. Unlike today, candidates who pandered to a narrow wing of their own party would have no chance whatsoever. They would be eliminated from contention.

Candidates who campaigned negatively would also be at a disadvantage. We wouldn't have to endure the kind of nasty battle between Senators Clinton and Obama that left many voters feeling embittered, feeling that the best person for the job of president had been knocked out of the race. With preferential elections, we also wouldn't have to choose between the lesser of two evils, as many of us felt we had to do in previous presidential contests.

On the contrary, with preferential elections, nearly all of us could justifiably feel that we'd had an excellent choice of candidates. And the vast majority of us could feel that the winner deserved to win.

As things now stand, though, there is one big obstacle to using preferential ballots in presidential races: Most of the time, no candidate would win a majority in the Electoral College. For instance, if the twelve candidates listed above were on the ballot in every state, several of those candidates would win some states, with the likely result that none of them would win a majority of electoral votes. Under the Constitution, the House of Representatives would then choose the president—which would defeat the whole purpose of using preferential ballots.

So to use preferential ballots in presidential elections, we'd need to amend the Constitution, replacing the Electoral College with one nationwide, popular election. Admittedly, that's a tall order. But now that San Francisco and other cities have adopted a preferential ballot for their municipal elections, the idea is sure to spread. In time, there could be wide support for electing presidents with preferential ballots.

Let's hope so. Only then will we have the best choices and be confident that the winner is the person whom most Americans want as their leader.

APPENDIX XIII

Q&A About Negotiations in a PAR House

Even in a PAR House, the majority would rule. So wouldn't minority voices be shut out?

Not likely, because lawmakers in the majority on some issues would wind up in the minority on other issues, so even the majority would want to trade across issues. For instance, conservatives have recently had enough power to substantially cut taxes. But conservatives are in the minority on the issue of abortion, so they have made little headway on that subject. In a PAR House, though, each lawmaker would want to achieve as much of his or her agenda as he or she could. So, conservatives might turn to the liberals and say, "We'll address your top concern on taxes if you'll accommodate us some on abortion."

What's more, in a PAR House, each lawmaker would represent a more coherent constituency. So, each one could explain to his or her constituents how they'd benefit from deals that he or she had struck with opponents. For instance, the Council on Sustainable Development struck "grand bargains" because each representative knew they were the most effective way to satisfy his or her own camp's thirst for progress.

Negotiations will occur behind closed doors. So, if a PAR legislator short-changed his or her constituents, how would voters ever know?

Most people would hold their representative accountable for results. He would have to explain how he'd achieved as much for them as was realistically possible. If his story didn't square with reality or if he was just covering up his own inadequacies, other candidates on his part of the spectrum would likely poke holes in his claims and show how they'd accomplish more.

Of course, challengers will find fault with any record. But the more a legislator distorted reality and the less he accomplished, the more ammunition he'd hand his opponents. Plus, voters with preferential ballots and many choices of candidates would be more likely to unseat legislators who delivered mediocre results.

In countries with more than two major parties, governments rise and fall more often than they do here. So if three parties had power in Congress, wouldn't it be less stable than now?

Most countries have a parliamentary system, in which a majority of the legislature picks the prime minister and thereby controls the entire government.* So the top priority of most lawmakers is to get into the majority and stay there. Meanwhile, lawmakers in the minority constantly try to destabilize the majority.

But the U.S. House doesn't control the whole government. So the priorities of U.S. lawmakers are somewhat different. Here, the typical legislator's top priority is reelection.

Still, every lawmaker wants power. So suppose that some PAR legislators tried to form a coalition that could control every issue. Each legislator asked to join might weigh the pros and cons this way:

"For this proposed coalition to prevail on any bill, we'd have to be nearly unanimous. Meanwhile, lawmakers outside the coalition would try to sabotage us as we sought support from the Senate and the president. The minority might also fight us in court.

"Alternatively, on each issue I care about, I could try to assemble as large a coalition as possible, in which every member would work to reach an agreement that would stick. Which way would I be better off? Which way would I fulfill more of the agenda my voters are counting on?"

By looking at politics today, we can see the answer to this question: When a large minority is gunning for you, you get less done than when you try to get the maximum number of allies on your side.

Would most PAR legislators make the smart choice? We won't know until PAR happens. But if voters didn't like what they saw, they'd boot out incumbents. Incumbents would eventually figure out the most productive course.

Kenneth Arrow won a Nobel Prize for proving that there's no ideal election system. So how can we claim that PAR is ideal?

---

* Appendix XIV.

No system is ideal because any system that meets one criterion very well is likely to fall short by other standards. For instance, the current system is more decisive than the alternatives (including PAR) because the majority party in Congress can prevail. But the current system is producing decisions that threaten our financial stability, our environment, our relations with the world, and even our survival.

By contrast, PAR is designed to motivate politicians to find practical solutions to pressing problems, more so than other systems. By that standard, PAR is superior to the alternatives.

By that same standard, America's current system was superior to what preceded it, but human beings designed it, so human beings learned how to exploit it. Won't people also figure out how to exploit PAR?

No doubt, but with PAR each voter could elect a representative on his or her own wavelength, so each of us would have more reason to hold our representative to account. With most of us paying more attention, PAR would be harder to manipulate than the current arrangement.

All the same, in time, some people will figure how to game PAR. So we will then have to modify it to deal with circumstances that we can't anticipate now.

Many ideologues on both the left and the right just want to prevail. They often refuse to negotiate. For instance, between 2001 and 2006, the political right had the upper hand. Since then, the left has been on the rise. Won't whoever is on top oppose PAR?

Here's our pitch to ideologues from any camp: Even when you're in the majority, you spend most of your resources trying to hold off the other side. You don't get to enact your platform without a fight. On most issues, you don't get to rescind all the existing legislation. You have to slog your way to each victory.

And when you have majority power, it's only temporary. The other side isn't going to give up the fight or shrink to a permanent minority. There are always some people who believe that government should help the disadvantaged, while others feel just as strongly that government ought to stay out of everyone's way. That's how this country has always been. In America's early years, for instance, Thomas Jefferson tried to limit the federal government's power, while Alexander Hamilton was determined to make the government very powerful. That ideological struggle will never end.

The best you can hope for is a mechanism for resolving your differences with ideological opponents in ways that best meet your needs and theirs. PAR would do that job better than other methods now in use.

Appendix XIV
Parliamentary Government

Some people advocate that the United States adopt parliamentary government, a process that most other democracies use. Under that structure, the legislature not only has the power to enact all laws, it also picks the chief executive.

To see the potential benefits of that arrangement, consider how it works in Britain: Each citizen gets to vote for one member of the House of Commons to represent the local district. That part is just like here. Once elected, though, the British House picks a prime minister (PM). If one political party wins a majority of seats, it usually elects its party leader as PM.

Citizens therefore tend to vote based on party leaders and party platforms, not local candidates. For instance, a British citizen who favors the Labor Party platform or who wants Labor Party leader Gordon Brown to remain as prime minister would likely vote for the district's Labor candidate, even if the voter thought little of that candidate. After all, if the Labor Party wins a majority of seats, it will control the whole government and can enact its platform in full.

On the other hand, if a party wins a majority but doesn't implement its platform, its voters will likely rebel at the next election. In other words, voters tend to hold their party to account for its promises.

In America, by contrast, most voters know that each lawmaker lacks the power to enact his or her platform. So, Americans rarely hold legislators to account for their campaign promises. To some, that difference makes parliamentary government superior to the American system.

However, under a parliamentary structure, the majority party in Congress would rule, with the power to pick the head of our government and enact any policy it chose. Our core principle of checks and balances would no longer operate. Congress would cease to be a place where opposing camps had any reason to work out their differences. We would essentially be abandoning the concept of deliberative democracy.

An election system that would encourage opposing camps to resolve their disagreements sensibly would be a better alternative.

Besides, to install parliamentary government, we would in effect have to tear up our Constitution and start over. That's not a serious possibility.

Appendix XV
Evaluating an Alternative Reform—
Initiatives and Referendums

Many states have made major decisions—such as enacting term limits—by referendum, so some people now advocate holding national referendums. That way, if politicians bungled or ignored problems that concern many of us, we could decide those issues ourselves.

That idea raises some troubling questions, though.

First, who would write the proposals that we'd all vote on? In most states, to put a subject up for a popular vote, some group has to gather enough signatures on a petition. The people usually motivated to launch petition drives are zealots for a particular cause. There's no mechanism to ensure that the measures everyone votes on are fair, sensible, or evenhanded.

What's more, if major national questions were decided by referendum, would most of us take the time to study the issues and the facts, to learn the ins and outs of each subject? Wouldn't most of us just vote our existing opinions? If so, the majority view, uninformed or not, would prevail. Is that progress?

Perhaps most troubling, referendums usually give voters a choice between two options. Two opposing sides butt heads. One side wins, the other loses. The clashing values and interests that made the underlying issue so controversial remain just as antagonistic as ever. The disagreement doesn't go away. One side simply overpowers the other.

On top of all that, in most referendums, the side that advertises the most has a big edge. Many referendums end up being decided by whoever has the deepest pocket.

Finally, suppose we could somehow frame balanced proposals and inform ourselves enough about the underlying issues to resolve them sensibly by referendum. Even so, lawmakers who made all the other decisions would still represent incoherent constituencies. Politicians' hearts and minds would still be gripped by the motives that rule them today.

In short, referendums cannot cure what ails our democracy.

Sources

Introduction

It was Mitt Romney's wife Ann, when he was governor of Massachusetts, who described Congress as "two guys in a canoe that is headed for the falls . . ." See "Contempt for Congress" by David S. Broder, *The Washington Post*, April 8, 2006.

Chapter 1

The narrative about the Council on Sustainable Development (CSD) is based on interviews with council co-chairs David Buzzelli and Jonathan Lash, plus the council's public report, *Sustainable America: A New Consensus for Prosperity, Opportunity, and a Healthy Environment for the Future* (Washington, DC: U.S. Government Printing Office, 1996). President Clinton created the council, so at the time it was known as the President's Council on Sustainable Development (PCSD). However, of the council's twenty-five members, only five held federal office, while nine members came from industry, seven from the environmental community, two from other interest groups, and two from state governments. The council operated like a representative body, independent of the administration. So, to avoid confusion about its role and operation, chapter 1 refers to it simply as the Council on Sustainable Development (CSD).

Information about the National Commission on Retirement Policy comes from its proposal, *The 21st Century Retirement Security Plan: The National Commission on Retirement Policy Final Report* (Washington, DC: Center for Strategic and International Studies, 1999).

The description of the National Commission on Energy Policy is based on its report, *Ending the Energy Stalemate: A Bipartisan Strategy to Meet America's Energy Challenges* and the website www.energycommission.org.

Information about the Common Ground Network for Life and Choice is based on an interview of its former director, Mary Jacksteit.

Information about negotiated rule-making comes from the *Negotiated Rulemaking Sourcebook* by David Pritzker and Deborah Dalton (Washington, DC: U.S. Government Printing Office, 1995).

CHAPTER 2

The concept of the efficient frontier was developed in the early 1900s by Italian economist Wilfredo Pareto. A fuller account of how the efficient frontier applies to negotiation can be found in Howard Raiffa's *The Art and Science of Negotiation* (Cambridge, MA: Harvard University Press, 1982).

The distinction between "positions" and "interests" as it affects the negotiation process comes from *Getting to Yes: Negotiating Agreement Without Giving In* by Roger Fisher and William Ury (New York: Houghton Mifflin, 1981).

More information on negotiation in multiparty disputes is available in *The Consensus Building Handbook*, edited by Lawrence Susskind, Sarah McKearnan, and Jennifer Thomas-Larmer (Thousand Oaks, CA: Sage Press, 2000).

CHAPTER 3

Facts about the Constitutional Convention were drawn from *1787: The Grand Convention* by Clinton Rossiter (New York: Macmillan, 1966).

CHAPTER 4

The account of a typical lawmaker's plight is based on interviews with former members of Congress, plus information from *Politics of Congressional Elections* by Gary C. Jacobson (Boston: Longman, 2008), *Congress and Its Members* by Roger H. Davidson and Walter J. Oleszek (Washington, DC: CQ Press, 2002), *Home Style: House Members in their Districts* by Richard F. Fenno Jr. (Boston: Little Brown, 1978), and *Congress: Keystone of the Washington Establishment* by Morris P. Fiorina (New Haven, CT: Yale University Press, 1989).

CHAPTER 6

The raw demographic data in this chapter comes from the DVD *108th Congressional District Summary Files: Census of Population and Housing* (Washington, DC: U.S. Census Bureau, 2003).

CHAPTER 7

The data on voter attitudes come from American National Election Studies (www.electionstudies.org) and from *noshows2000*, a report issued by the Medill School of Journalism at Northwestern University (www.yvoteonline.org/noshows2000.shtml).

That one-winner per-district elections create voter apathy is well known to many advocates for proportional representation. For example, see *Real Choices/New Voices: The Case for Proportional Representation Elections in the United States* by Douglas J. Amy (New York: Columbia University Press, 1993.)

The story about the Ford assembly line comes from "What's Creating an 'Industrial Miracle' at Ford," *Business Week*, July 30, 1984, pp. 80-81.

CHAPTER 8

The Newt Gingrich quote comes from "Big Business Learns to Live With Newt" by Ann Reilly Dowd, *Fortune*, September 18, 1995, p. 116.

The data on farm subsidies come from the Department of Agriculture and the Congressional Budget Office. The analysis also draws on "Top 10 Reasons to Veto the Farm Bill" by Brian M. Riedl at the Heritage Foundation (www.heritage.org/Research/Budget/BG1538.cfm), April 17, 2002.

CHAPTER 9

The 2006 Annual Report of the Board of Trustees of the Federal Hospital Insurance and Federal Supplementary Medical Insurance Trust Funds estimated Medicare's total unfunded liabilities at $70 trillion. Since then, the trustees have reported just the deficit for the next seventy-five years. The 2008 annual report estimated that figure to be $36.3 trillion.

The estimate that adequately protecting against nuclear terrorism would cost five to ten billion dollars a year comes from *Nuclear Terrorism: The Ultimate Preventable Catastrophe* by Graham Allison (New York: Times Books, 2004), p. 177.

CHAPTER 10

The information about proportional representation (PR) in the United States comes from *Proportional Representation and Electoral Reform in Ohio* edited by Kathleen Barber (Columbus: Ohio State University Press, 1995) and by Douglas J. Amy's *Real Choices/New Voices* (see chapter 7 above).

However, the analysis of PR's flaws is based on our experience in mediating public policy disputes. Our conclusions differ from both Barber's and Amy's.

The claim in this chapter that America's most prominent advocates for PR cannot cite another country that most Americans would consider a model of better policymaking is based on a real event. At a conference to promote PR in the United States, held in Boston in November 1995, we asked the PR advocates on the podium if they could name any such country. Many of them responded—some at length—but no one answered the question. Several times that weekend, the head of the sponsoring organization said publicly, "We need to come up with an answer." However, they didn't.

APPENDIX I

The story about the National Commission on Superfund is based on an interview with the NCS chair, Jonathan Lash, plus the commission's Final Consensus Report (1994).

The story about the New York City watershed agreement comes from multiple articles that appeared in the *New York Times* (www.nytimes.com) between 1996 and 2004.

APPENDIX III

The demographic data is from the U.S. Census. However, the early Census collected far less data than it does now. So as noted in the graphs, some information is extrapolated backward in time.

The information on home values in the eighteenth century comes from *Distribution of Wealth and Income in the United States in 1798* by Lee Soltow (Pittsburgh: University of Pittsburgh Press, 1989).

APPENDIX IV

The quotes are drawn from the version of *The Federalist* assembled by Jacob

Cooke at Wesleyan University in 1961, published by Bantam in 1982, and edited by Gary Wills. Wills notes that Madison's manuscripts have disappeared and that Cooke obtained Madison's contributions to *The Federalist* from the New York newspapers in which they were first published.

Appendix VII

The information about election systems is drawn from *Electoral System Design: The New International IDEA Handbook* (Stockholm: International Institute for Democracy and Electoral Assistance, 2005). The analysis of those systems, however, is ours.

ACKNOWLEDGMENTS

Fitst and foremost, we want to thank Rebecca Behrends. For the last two years of this book's evolution, she has been our muse, our sounding board, and our principal editor. She has given us unending moral and practical support. To each page, she added color, clarity, and heart. We don't have sufficient words for the contribution she has made.

At the start of this process, Kat Matlick was our mainstay. She helped us turn ideas into coherent words. She edited many articles and early drafts of the manuscript. She helped us gather outside resources when needed. She believed in us and our mission through good times and bad.

When we began to write, several professionals lent their expertise. David Kohn helped us build this book's structure, chapter by chapter. Karl Weber and Bob Reiser showed us how to make the manuscript a more engaging read. Richard Berman helped turn our information into a coherent story. Doug Magee generated many imaginative ideas for enlivening the dialogue and maintaining momentum. Barry Fox and Ralph Sell helped research the material in chapters 4 and 5. Martin Roper helped us turn our rough manuscript into a lucid whole.

Jerrold Mundis then served as the ideal coach to help us turn all we'd done into a genuine book. He edited, he advised, he encouraged. He was both a fan and a voice of reality. He and Charles Young did the next to final edit.

Many friends and supporters contributed time, encouragement, and valuable suggestions. We are eternally grateful to Morris Propp, Cindy Franklin,

Tony Hagar, Tim Dwight, Stephanie Phillips, Bill Redpath, Dave Watts, Claudia Newman, Ted Gutierrez, Charney Bromberg, Ivan Wolff, Abby Glasser, Jerry Greenberg, Ellen Hazen, Gene Brody, Karl Trautman, Gerry Eichner, Marie Margenau-Spatz, Richard Eric Spatz, Harold Erdman, Larry Spears, Thomas Moore, Vince Hyman, David Skaggs, Charles Euchner, Dick Hersh, David Deering, Melissa Smith, Justin Behrends, David Tereschuk, Steve Crandall, Barbara Joel, Laura Gray, Paul Silverman, Ian Cervone, Bob Jenks, Judith Appelbaum, Beverly Schanzer, Janet Walsh, Margaret Lichtenberg, Frank Sander, Michael Wheeler, Linda Cashden, Michael Larsen, Farley Chase, Rafe Sagalyn, Eric Lupfer, Ted Weinstein, Marilyn Allen, and Coleen O'Shea.

Lastly, we want to thank Hilary Claggett, our editor at Potomac Books, for her penetrating suggestions and unending patience in bringing this book to completion.

INDEX

About the Authors

Sol Erdman is the founder and president of the Center for Collaborative Democracy (CCD). He became an expert on resolving political conflict by first becoming adept at conflict itself. His first career was on Wall Street, an environment that Erdman describes as "one of the most highly evolved forms of aggression known to mankind—the right place for me in my twenties and thirties." In that time frame, he rose to senior vice president and head of options arbitrage at Oppenheimer & Company.

At midlife, however, Erdman was drawn to the idea of resolving difficult conflicts. Attending the Program on Negotiation at Harvard Law School, he was soon doing independent research with some of its leading thinkers. By studying their methods for resolving bitter disputes, Erdman discerned what it would take to coax elected officials to resolve their differences on highly contentious issues.

To disseminate this new approach, Erdman founded CCD in 1995. He has presented its innovative methods to the Council of State Governments, members of Congress, the American Political Science Association, and leading pundits. Erdman's articles, with Lawrence Susskind, have appeared in *State Government News, Roll Call,* the *Boston Globe,* the *Chicago Tribune,* and the *Los Angeles Times.*

Lawrence Susskind is the Ford Professor of Urban and Environmental Planning at the Massachusetts Institute of Technology, director of the MIT-Harvard Public Disputes Program, and vice chair of the Program on Negotiation at

Harvard Law School. He has been teaching advanced courses on negotiation for more than twenty years. In 1993 he helped create the Consensus Building Institute, where he has mediated national policy debates, refereed regional political battles, and helped mediate international treaties, including the Kyoto Protocol on global warming.

Susskind is the author of eighteen books, two of which have won "best dispute resolution book of the year" awards: *Dealing With an Angry Public* (Free Press) and *The Consensus Building Handbook* (Sage). He is also the winner of the prestigious Educator of the Year Award from the American Planning Association and the Pioneer Award from the Society for Professionals in Dispute Resolution. For more information see www.lawrencesusskind.com and www.cbuilding.org.